insight text guide

Dominic Lennard

The Man Who Loved Children

Christina Stead

First published in 2015, reprinted in 2017.

Insight Publications Pty Ltd
3/350 Charman Road
Cheltenham VIC 3192
Australia
Tel: +61 3 8571 4950
Fax: +61 3 8571 0257
Email: books@insightpublications.com.au

www.insightpublications.com.au

National Library of Australia Cataloguing-in-Publication entry:
Lennard, Dominic, author.
Christina Stead's The man who loved children / Dominic Lennard.
9781925316063 (paperback)
Insight text guides
Includes bibliographical references.
Stead, Christina, 1902–1983.—Criticism and interpretation.
Stead, Christina, 1902–1983. Man who loved children.
Australian fiction—20th century—History and criticism.
A823.4

Other ISBNs:
9781925316070 (digital)
9781925316087 (bundle: print + digital)

Cover design: The Modern Art Production Group

Printed in Australia

contents

Character map iv

Overview 1

- About the author 1
- Synopsis 2
- Character summaries 4

Background & context 6

Genre, structure & language 9

Chapter-by-chapter analysis 15

Characters & relationships 32

Themes, ideas & values 45

Different interpretations 56

Questions & answers 61

Sample answer 70

References & reading 73

CHARACTER MAP

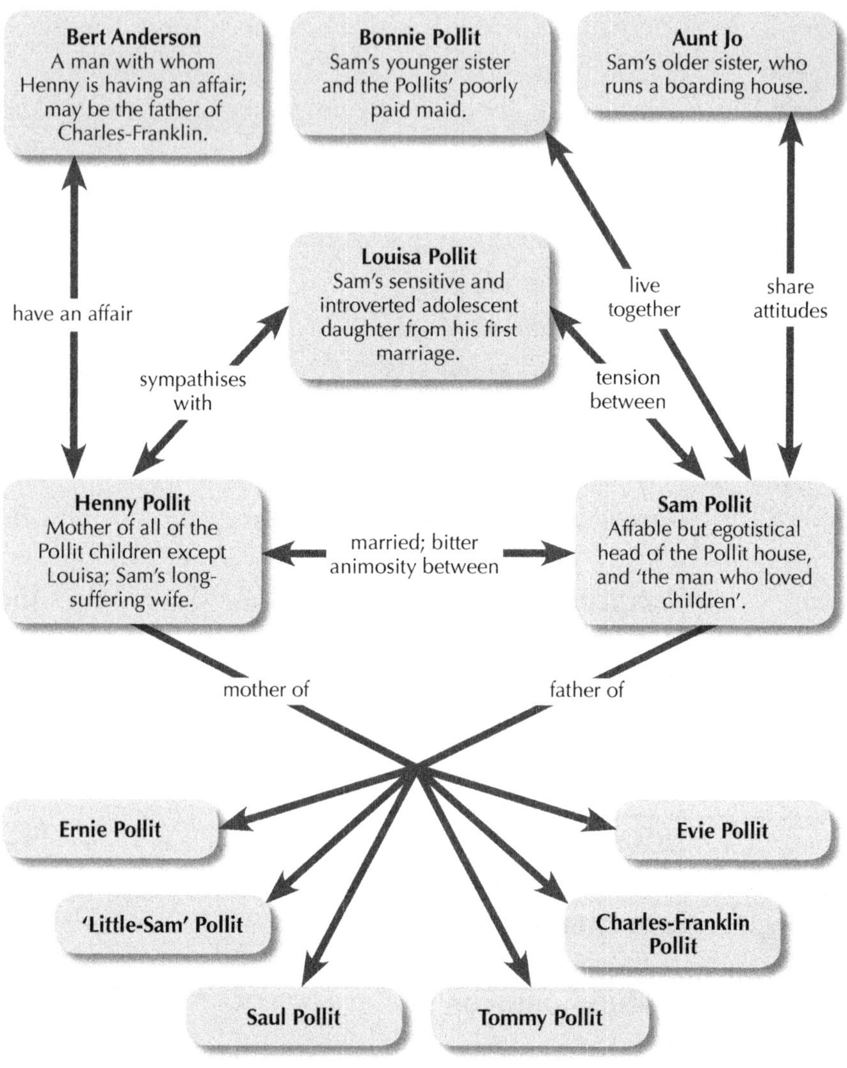

OVERVIEW

About the author

Christina Stead was born in Sydney in 1902. Stead's conservationist father, David, is widely known to have inspired her portrayal of Sam Pollit in *The Man Who Loved Children*. Stead's mother died when she was two (like Louisa in the novel), and her father remarried. She followed her father's fascination with the natural world and considered herself a naturalist. This preoccupation with nature informed her writing, as she often focused on the intricacies of daily life, a style clearly on display in *The Man Who Loved Children*. However, after she left Australia in 1928, she never saw her father again. She spent the majority of her life away from her home country, living in France, England and the United States.

As with her portrayal of Sam Pollit, Stead was known to draw upon her friends and family in her depiction of fictional characters. She authored fifteen novels, including *For Love Alone* (1945) and *Letty Fox: Her Luck* (1946). She also worked as a screenwriter during the 1940s, contributing to John Ford's war film *They Were Expendable* (1945). However, *The Man Who Loved Children* remains her best-known and most celebrated work. While the novel was originally set in Sydney, Stead's publisher encouraged her to change it to an American setting; she also altered the time period from 1914–15 to the late 1930s. The novel was not widely read until it was reprinted in 1965 with an introduction by the poet and critic Randall Jarrell, after which critical appreciation rose markedly. *The Man Who Loved Children* has been taught in Australian schools, and today Stead is considered an important contributor to Australia's literary history.

Christina Stead spent her final years in Australia, living in Canberra, Sydney and Melbourne, before she died in 1983. In 2010, *The Man Who Loved Children* was selected as one of *TIME*'s top 100 novels published since 1923.

Synopsis

The novel is set in the Baltimore–Washington area in the late 1930s. Henrietta ('Henny') Pollit and her husband Sam arrive separately to their home, Tohoga House, where they live with their six children, whose ages range from four to twelve. Sam's younger sister, Bonnie, also lives with the family. Henny and Sam differ greatly in manner and in their approach to parenting, and we learn that they have for years been locked in an intense rivalry with each other. Henny is from a wealthy family, and her money helps sustain the Pollits, but she receives a letter that indicates the family's deep financial strife.

Conflict between Sam and Henny breaks out over breakfast, and fights between them continue to erupt throughout the novel. Henny feels trapped, downtrodden and dispirited by marriage and life in the house. Sam sees himself as honest and long-suffering, and cannot understand his wife's hostility; yet he is egotistical and oblivious to the suffering of others. Louisa (Louie), the eldest child, is the daughter from Sam's first marriage. Although verbally and sometimes physically abused by Henny, Louisa begins to see why her eccentric and volatile stepmother might behave as she does, and increasingly comes to resent her father's control and ignorance.

Louisa visits one of her neighbours, Mrs Kydd, and kills a cat for her, an act she hopes in vain will connect her to a female figure outside the house. Henny travels to Baltimore to meet Bert Anderson, a man with whom she is having an affair. While Henny is downtown, Sam's older sister, Jo, visits the Pollits to reprimand Bonnie, who works as a maid for the family, over an affair she is having with a married man. During these events, tension increases between Louisa and her father. Sam sees Louisa as the child closest to him, yet he also teases her over her appearance and introversion, especially when she contradicts him.

Since it is the first week of summer holidays, Louisa goes to stay with the family of her deceased mother, the Bakens, at a place called Harpers Ferry, where she feels a sense of inclusion. After Henny collects her, they travel to Monocacy, Henny's family home, which is in disrepair as the family's finances gradually run out. Exchanges between Henny, her mother and her sisters indicate that the problems Henny has with her egotistical husband are shared by many women.

While in Malaya for work, Sam has a falling-out with a colleague that sets in motion the gradual undoing of his career. Upon returning, Sam's influence on the house appears to have weakened. Henny is heavily pregnant with yet another child, and when she receives notice that her father has died, the financial position of the Pollits plummets further. With characteristic pride and self-righteousness, Sam refuses to address damaging rumours about himself that are being spread by his colleagues, compounding his situation and the family's financial strain. Eventually, the family sells Tohoga House and moves into a rundown dwelling by the river that they call 'Spa House'.

Louisa develops a fascination with a new teacher, Miss Aiden, who becomes an intelligent and optimistic female role model for her. Conflict between Louisa and Sam occurs repeatedly. He refuses to let her move out and continues to manipulate her emotionally, claiming that he wants Louisa to think for herself, while denying her independence. Sam remains persistently oblivious to the misery of those around him. Miss Aiden is invited to dinner; however, the narcissistic Sam makes himself the centre of attention, upsetting Louisa.

An anonymous note addressed to Sam tells him that his youngest son, Charles-Franklin, is not his, but the result of Henny's affair. This further increases tension between Sam and his wife. Henny begins to make arrangements to leave Sam, but Bert abandons her when he hears that the affair has been discovered. Feeling the house to be an endless trap, Louisa decides to kill her father and mother by poisoning their tea. However, she panics as she puts her plan into action, and only one cup is laced. Henny, who has threatened suicide throughout the novel, intuits what her stepdaughter has done and drinks the poisoned tea, dying quickly. After Henny's death, Sam further inflates himself as heroic in his suffering, and Louisa is expected to take over the maternal role. Instead, she runs away, achieving her independence.

Character summaries

Samuel Pollit

Sam is the husband of Henny and the father of the children. He is cheerful but self-centred, and over-confident of his own intelligence and judgement.

Henny (Henrietta) Pollit

Henny is Sam's wife and the mother of all his children except Louisa. Originally from a wealthy Baltimore family, she is angry and eccentric, frustrated by her husband's ignorance and the life into which she feels locked.

Louisa (Louie) Pollit

Louisa is Sam's twelve-year-old daughter. She is artistic and introverted. Despite her stepmother's hostility towards her, Louisa is sympathetic to Henny because she can see how a male-dominated society, and Henny's husband Sam, have ground her down.

Ernest (Ernie) Pollit

Ernie is one of the Pollit children, younger than Louisa. He is meticulous with his money and greatly interested in financial matters.

Evie Pollit

Evie is the second-eldest daughter, after Louisa. She is eight years old at the start of the novel. Sam refers to her by the pet name, 'Little Womey' ('Little Woman').

Bonnie Pollit

Bonnie is Sam's younger sister. She is twenty-five years old and lives with the Pollits, working as the family's poorly paid maid.

Aunt Josephine

Aunt Josephine, or Aunt Jo, is Sam Pollit's older sister. She is middle-aged and runs a local boarding house. She is very concerned with social appearances.

Bert Anderson

Bert is Henny's lover and works for the Department of Internal Revenue. He lives for immediate gratification and is without Sam's philosophical pretence.

Miss Aiden

Miss Aiden is a teacher at Louisa's school. Lacking other positive female role models, Louisa is attracted to and fascinated by this intelligent woman.

Aunt Hassie

Aunt Hassie is Henny's sister and the mother of Cathy. She lives in Baltimore.

Saul Pilgrim

Saul is Sam's oldest friend. He advises Sam to address the rumours about him.

Clare Meredith

Clare is a poverty-stricken schoolfriend of Louisa's. She is outgoing and full of jokes, yet ultimately feels trapped by her circumstances.

BACKGROUND & CONTEXT

Setting

The novel draws heavily on Stead's childhood and her strained relationship with her father, and was originally set in Sydney in the early years of World War I. However, it was rewritten to take place in the Baltimore–Washington area in the late 1930s (thus causing some early reviewers to complain about geographical and linguistic inaccuracies). Consequently, its time frame covers the later years of the Great Depression and the lead-up to World War II.

In Chapter Six, as part of his work Sam ventures to Malaya, otherwise known as British Malaya. 'Malaya' referred to Singapore and the British-controlled states of the Malay Archipelago. After World War II, many of these states formed the federation of Malaysia.

The Prohibition era

The novel is set shortly after the Prohibition era in the United States, of which several mentions are made. This period, which lasted from 1920 to 1933, involved a nationwide ban on the production and sale of alcoholic beverages. Sam, a staunch anti-drinker, romanticises the presidency of Franklin D Roosevelt, who held office during this era. Sam refuses to allow alcohol in the house, although Henny has a bottle hidden in her room. Activism to bring about Prohibition focused on preventing the social ills of alcohol, including domestic violence, and on alcohol's perceived threat to family values. Consequently, it is ironic that, while the Pollit household is virtually alcohol-free due to Sam's moral objection, it is boiling over with abuse and disunity.

The Great Depression

The novel is set during the final years of the Great Depression, a period of global economic downturn that ran from 1929 to 1939. The spectre of poverty is present early in the narrative, when Bonny accidentally burns Henny's blouse, sending her into a rage (p.51). Later, Ernie is surprised to find that Henny has sold many personal items to keep up with expenses. Henny is part of a society family of wealthy industrialists, the Collyers; however, that fortune has gradually dwindled, and by the time of her father's death the Pollit home must be sold. In light of the difficult financial circumstances of the time, Sam's unwillingness to defend his reputation and hold onto his job seems especially naive and selfish.

Patriarchy

The novel is set in a period during which patriarchal power – the centring of family, social and political life around male interests – was deeply entrenched. Women had only received voting rights in the United States in 1920, and lacked significant political representation. Sam assumes himself to be head of the Pollit household, and the reason he and Henny have so many children seems primarily because he ('the man who loved children') wants them. Henny does not have a job; her role is primarily child-rearing, and she is largely confined to the domestic sphere. Similarly, the majority of housework is done by Sam's female children, especially Louisa, but also Evie, whom he refers to as 'Little Womey' – his 'little woman'. Interests and opportunities for women beyond the roles of wife and mother are restricted. Louisa is partly characterised by her imagination and soaring artistic talents; yet, until she meets Miss Aiden (see p.131), she has not been exposed to female role models who might inspire her.

Divorce

The animosity between Henny and Sam probably strikes readers as surprisingly explosive and uncomfortable – indeed, intolerable. While in today's world Henny might have sought to divorce Sam, saving them both further misery, during the period in which the novel is set, divorce was not easy to initiate – particularly for a woman. In order to divorce one's spouse, one needed to show a decisive cause, such as cruelty or adultery. Consequently, Henny complains in Chapter Five that Sam's virtuousness in this regard actually keeps her trapped (p.175).

However, as a woman, Henny's life is structured around her home and family, with few opportunities beyond the domestic sphere. Consequently, once news of the affair breaks, Henny is terrified that Sam – having evidence of a legally adequate cause for divorce – will use the affair to leave Henny and deprive her of her children.

GENRE, STRUCTURE & LANGUAGE

The Man Who Loved Children is a challenging novel. It immerses the reader in the world of the Pollits at great length and in significant detail, and that world is frequently bleak and confronting. Sam often speaks to his children in an infantile dialect that may strike readers as off-putting, but is effective in increasing our discomfort with him, as well as amplifying the sense of emotional suffocation within the house. Henny repeatedly raves and threatens, and the skirmishes between the couple mire us in a family life that, while dramatic in its bitterness, does not seem to offer its characters any real release or resolution. Given the novel's length, this content can make for difficult reading; however, it also allows us to experience the world of the Pollits in all its toxicity, frustration and despair.

Genre

Realism and naturalism

The Man Who Loved Children can be broadly located within a tradition of **realism**, although with some qualifications. Realist writing seeks to depict the world 'as it really is' – to focus largely on familiar, everyday life. Certainly Stead's novel focuses on the everyday, and while its characters may command our interest with their Shakespearean-like tragedies, they and the world in which they live and interact are not foreign or exotic. The novel's emphasis on family poverty and restriction means that it might be further located within a *social-realist* tradition: works focused on highlighting oppressive conditions that structure the lives of the middle and lower classes.

The novel also shares some characteristics of **naturalism**, an outgrowth of realism. Like realism, naturalism seeks to depict the world realistically, avoiding melodrama, but it is also often pessimistic in outlook, eschews the convention of a single 'heroic' character, and has a large number of minor characters (which *The Man Who Loved Children* certainly does). In its focus on vicious marital antipathy and domestic violence, the novel also accords with naturalism's focus on 'darker' topics that breach social decorum. Naturalism emphasises disempowered characters who do not necessarily change greatly throughout the course of a novel, and characters who are shaped by their social circumstances. Consistent with this idea, much of the misery of the characters in *The Man Who Loved Children* stems from Henny's and Sam's essentially unchanging natures, and consequently their unending conflict. Additionally, Henny, of course, is significantly disempowered within the novel (trapped by the profound failure of her marriage); in the tradition of naturalism, her bitter and unstable personality is strongly influenced by her environment.

Modern Gothic

Although the novel's everyday setting and its insistence on capturing the minutiae of life in the Pollit house bear many of the characteristics of realism and naturalism, the novel's events can sometimes seem overblown or perverse in manner that evokes the 'excesses' of Gothic literature. Traditionally Gothic texts feature atmospheres of suspense and mystery, and may take place in rundown houses or medieval settings. They also feature high emotion, and characters with warped or tyrannical mindsets.

In this novel, the traditionally Gothic rundown house is replaced by a house ground down through poverty and neglect, and Sam Pollit can be seen as an updated version of the male tyrant of a Gothic novel such as Horace Walpole's *The Castle of Otranto*. *The Man Who Loved Children*'s depiction of seething antagonism can also be seen as a modern, domestic reworking of the Gothic's focus on dark, perverse mindsets and overwrought emotion. As a form of Romanticism, the Gothic strains the limits of realism by emphasising the sensational and grotesque. For instance, at one point the narrator describes Henny's 'huge eyeball in its glove of flesh, deep-sunk in the wrinkled skullhole, the dark circle round it and the eyebrow far above' (p.4), a description that seems to overemphasise her grotesque physicality.

The conflict between Henny and Sam sometimes strains plausibility too in a way that befits the Gothic. Sam's degree of self-importance is almost incredible, while Henny's volatile behaviour is striking. The novel seems to fluctuate between the realistic and the darkly sensational: as readers, we might be confronted with an 'abnormal' event that is embedded within the realistic and everyday, or an everyday reality that slips into the almost unbelievable. This allows us to contemplate the dramatic aspects of everyday life structured by social forces such as male power: forces that ordinarily, in the society in which the novel is set, remain hidden. While the world of the novel seems 'normal', or even banal, Stead's use of this Gothic excess shows us the darkness and abnormality lurking beneath.

Coming-of-age story

The Man Who Loved Children can be read as a coming-of-age story focused on the eldest daughter, Louisa. The coming-of-age tale (often referred to as a bildungsroman) depicts a young protagonist transitioning to an 'adult' identity through a series of challenges, and often a central moral decision. Examples of this type of work include *Jane Eyre* (1847), *To Kill a Mockingbird* (1960), the Harry Potter series (1997–2007) and the film *Life of Pi* (2012). The coming-of-age story is often referred to as a 'genre'; however, like most genres it rarely exists in isolation, and it is common for coming-of-age themes to be included in texts from a variety of different genres (musicals, gangster films and so on).

Coming-of-age protagonists are typically sensitive and isolated in their family or social environment. In their journey to adulthood, they are often left to their own devices, needing to demonstrate independence, resolve and sound judgement. In *The Man Who Loved Children*, Louisa is introverted and disconnected from her family, especially her father. She has grand artistic ambitions and a strong sense of her own potential, but neither are likely to be realised within the suffocating environment in which she lives. The novel partly focuses on her attempts to challenge and break away from her domineering father's influence. Perversely, perhaps, Louisa's most dramatic moment of decision-making comes when she decides to murder both of her parents in order to escape from the spirit-crushing monotony of the house. Although she only partially succeeds in her aim, by the novel's conclusion she feels her childhood is gone forever, and she is able to make the decision to leave the Pollit house for good.

Structure

The long novel is divided into ten chapters, although each one is punctuated by section breaks with headings that loosely indicate the focus of the narrative to follow. The novel covers a period of approximately three years, but the first four chapters (around 150 pages) are dedicated to covering only around forty-eight hours in the life of the Pollits. This extended start means that we are plunged into and held under the suffocating world of the family, experiencing the minutiae of lives that fluctuate between ordinary and disturbing.

Language

Stead writes with a keen eye for seemingly insignificant details that work to greatly enhance the realism of the novel. The text is also peppered with descriptions of the environment around the Pollit houses (the weather, flora and wildlife), which creates a sense of a vibrant natural world to contrast with the stifling psychological drama within the house – and sometimes to reflect that drama (e.g. the electrical storm towards the end of the novel).

In general, Stead works to embed her characters within a rich and detailed reality of their social and physical circumstances. Readers will also notice that the heavy use of slang, pet names and other unusual words helps to create an impression of an isolated and particular family world with its own language. Since it is Sam who primarily utilises and defines this language, language itself is an important signifier of his power within the household (discussed further in 'Themes, Ideas & Values').

Point of view

The novel is narrated in the third person, and so does not tie us to any one character's particular point of view. The text generally strives to depict characters' interactions objectively: Stead describes exchanges without intrusive authorial comment or judgement, allowing readers to form their own opinion of the characters; however, occasionally a character's behaviour may be noted ironically or sarcastically, especially Sam's. For example, as Sam admires Maryland, the state in which he lives, the narration states that 'he made a great many other remarks which proved that it was only after a strict examination of all the other states in the Union, he had impartially chosen the Free State to be born in' (p.310).

Throughout *The Man Who Loved Children* Stead uses a narrative technique known as **free indirect speech**, which allows us to imagine the world of the text from multiple perspectives. Although the narration does not restrict our viewpoint to that of a single character, it adopts various characters' points of view on different occasions. For instance, Stead writes:

> Henny smirked even more, seeing this wildcat, hedgerow, wild-weed, slum-artisan, cheap-Baltimore family grow more jolly ... Bonny (obviously sleeping with some man who was doing her dirt) and Jinny (whose pert daughter Essie needed her face slapped) and Jo (whose hair was like a haystack in a fit) and all their weedy, rank children getting merrier and merrier on the dungheap that was their life. (p.260)

While Henny is not narrating in the first person, the narrator has temporarily adopted her perspective, allowing us access to her thoughts.

Louisa is the character whose interiority is most developed and whom we most get to know through her thoughts being revealed to us (and surely the character with whom we identify most closely). Our focus on

Louisa's internal life is developed in the opening chapter, through her vision of the 'night rider' (p.22), and also in her growing identification with her stepmother at the end of the chapter (pp.34–5). This signals Louisa as a character with transformative potential, while her parents largely remain unchanged throughout the novel.

CHAPTER-BY-CHAPTER ANALYSIS

Chapter One (pp.1–35)

Summary: *Henny and Sam arrive home separately. Their characters and their bitter rivalry is described. Through a letter addressed to Henny, it is revealed that the family are under financial strain. On Sunday morning, Sam spends time with the children.*

The novel opens with Louisa minding the Pollit children. She hears them playing as she goes about solitary activities, which hints at her introverted nature. She is 'benevolent' when left in charge but 'strict and anxious' (p.1) when her parents are home, suggesting the tension of the Pollit house.

Henny arrives and is 'seen from various corners by the perspiring young ones', who 'rushed to meet her' (p.1). The initial descriptions of Henny emphasise her changeable mood: she snaps at her children, 'Are you catching flies?' but 'then she would be cheerful' (p.3). This changeability suggests an ambivalence towards her maternal role – her combination of love for the children and resentment of her confinement.

In contrast, as the cheerful Sam makes his way home the imagery is positive, suggesting his re-entry into a domain in which he feels a sense of belonging and control. The streets are described as a 'little island ... between river and parks'. As the children in the street 'went shouting, colliding downhill', Sam 'came up whistling', both comfortable with and implicitly part of the childish frivolity around him. Sam talks to himself as he walks, appraising his progress in life and coaching himself to further greatness. With clichéd zest, he says he is 'going to glory' and that he has 'come a long way, a long, long way' (p.15). His jaunty pride contrasts with his wife's feelings of dissatisfaction and stagnation, and his focus on himself indicates the ignorance at the centre of his character – his self-absorption and indifference to the feelings of those around him.

Sam has been contemplating an affair, though he feels the need to suppress this desire: 'the love that harms another is not love' (p.16). But as soon as he renounces interest in Madeleine, his secretary, his attention is diverted to Gillian Roebuck – 'a child-woman' with 'an innocent, attentive face' (p.16). This indicates that Sam's moralism is conflicted and hypocritical; he notes, despite his intentions, 'what desires beset a man!' (p.16). Moreover, the language used to describe Gillian indicates Sam's attraction to women who are childlike and deferential, and thus flatter his power. Similarly, Sam later puts on symptoms of a stomach-ache to gain Louisa's attention, 'begging her, yearning after her' (p.28). This uncomfortably sexual language indicates the inappropriateness of Sam's relationship to his female children, as he asks of them the attention he does not get from his wife.

While Henny's view of the world reveals her misanthropy, Sam's reveals his idealism. Henny sees the society around her as bestial and repulsive, filled with 'creatures' governed by base instinct. Her descriptions of people rely on grotesque animal imagery; she describes, for instance, 'a dirty shrimp of a man with a fishy expression who purposely leaned over [her]' (p.6). In contrast to Henny's perception of a world filled with revolting caricatures, Sam's world view is more 'high-minded' (p.7). 'Mother Earth,' he notes, 'I love you, I love men and women, I love little children and all innocent things' (p.19). This disparity in views indicates the power relationship between the two, and their differing social power. Henny feels depressed and worn out by the world, so, unlike her husband, she sees it as obscene and confronting.

In her increasing dissatisfaction with her father's dominance, Louisa looks favourably on the defiant Henny. Contemplating Henny's experiences, she links them with those of women generally: 'For it was not Henny alone who went through this inferno, but every woman' (p.8). This indicates one of the novel's key themes: the experiences of women in a male-dominated society. Stead describes Louisa's comprehension of her stepmother's point of view; Henny has become 'a creature of flesh and blood, nearer to Louisa because, like the little girl, she was guilty, rebellious, and got chastised' (p.33).

When Henny attacks Louisa, the girl looks 'up into her stepmother's face, squirming, but not trying to get away, questioning her silently, needing to understand, in an affinity of misfortune' (p.18). This demonstrates Louisa's desire to identify with her stepmother based on their shared feelings of oppression. Louisa 'admir[es] Henny for her strength of mind' (p.8), and for her implicit critique of Sam's power and control. Louisa understands that Henny's antagonism towards Sam is the 'hate of woman the house-jailed and child-chained against the keycarrier' (p.34).

On Sunday morning, Sam tells Evie that a story he has been reading 'comes to a good end' because, despite the characters' acrimony, they 'really love each other, although they *do* show a tendency to scratch each other's eyes at moments' (p.26). This an example of a *mise-en-abyme*: a 'text within a text' that mirrors the themes or events of the novel as a whole. Sam uses the story to express his confidence in his belief that the rancour in the Pollit family is ultimately subservient to love. However, the mirroring is ironic: the novel doesn't, as Sam would have it, come 'to a good end' (p.26), and while he may claim to love others unconditionally, he is blind to their disaffection.

Key point

Henny and Sam are bitterly at odds. The thoughtful and introspective Louisa, despite being neglected by her stepmother, is becoming old enough to understand that Henny is not as 'crazy' as she seems, but that her unhappiness has justification.

Q Make a list of characteristics of each parent. How do their personalities differ?

Chapter Two (pp.36–68)

Summary: *Conflict between Henny and Sam breaks out over breakfast, and Louisa's resentment of her father grows. Bonny accidentally burns one of Henny's blouses, further revealing the family's financial strain.*

For the amusement of her youngest son, Tommy, Henny sings a song about Polly the parrot, which evokes the family's surname, 'Pollit' (p.37). A parrot, who repeats words it has been taught, can be seen as symbolic of the children's stiuation: Sam expects them to serve as an audience and to echo his own ideas. Additionally, pet parrots are kept caged and/or have their wings clipped – an apt metaphor for Henny, as well as for Louisa, who both feel confined by Sam.

During breakfast, Louisa recites quotations learned at her father's behest that advise on becoming a 'great man' (p.41). Sam suggests that one quotation applies to women as well as men, but Louisa points out that it does not mention women. Sam accuses Louisa of not understanding the quotations and not appreciating 'her pore little dad' (p.42).

Key point

This is an instance of irony within the text: in identifying that the quotations do not include women, Louisa intimates that the society in which the Pollits live is not constructed to benefit female greatness, only that of men. In this, she demonstrates a level of comprehension that Sam himself does not possess. Moreover, in suggesting that Louisa does not 'appreciate' him, Sam turns the focus back to himself, unwittingly reinforcing the idea that men are always the focus of attention.

Sam confides that he dreamt he was in a forest of snakes, noting 'bad sign! Snakes mean enemies!' (p.43). This foreshadows Louisa's play later in the novel, 'The Snake-Man', in which the father is cast as a dangerous snake. Sam describes the snakes in his dream as obstructing his path, but it is clear to the reader that it is Sam who consistently obstructs Louisa, repeatedly denying her a life beyond his direct influence.

Claiming he is tired of the family's disunity, Sam instructs Louisa to tell Henny to join them for breakfast. His use of the term 'Pet' (p.43) for Henny reinforces the imagery of imprisoned animals. Henny is resentful of being ordered to listen to her husband's 'mawkery', claiming that 'he has enough of an audience' (p.43). This scene provides an example of Sam's inadequate attempt to fix the deep rift between Henny and himself. He demands unity: 'I will not tolerate this everlasting schism' (p.43). But in doing so, he only reinforces the power dynamic that Henny resents, thereby exacerbating the problem (and Henny's resentment) rather than addressing it.

Sam tries to attract neighbourhood children to the house; he is clearly 'the man who loved children' of the novel's title. However, he 'did not care for the girls of school age as much as for the baby girls' (p.45). From this the reader can infer that Sam sees younger children as more susceptible to his charms and projected sense of his own importance. This reinforces the notion that Sam likes to surround himself with female figures who are compliant, adoring and easily impressed.

Sam grandly articulates to the children his views of the 'brotherhood' of man. His language is sexist, although it is worth noting that it was the norm to use 'man' to signify humankind during the period in which the novel was written. Nevertheless, given Louisa's earlier critique of this exclusionary language, Sam's extensive references to 'male' fellowship stand out and reinforce the ignorance that underlies his philosophising. He also laments the limitations in how women are raised: 'that is the curse of the bringing-up of women to useless arts. They used to be brought up to catch men ... women have been brought up much like slaves, that is, to lie' (pp.59–60). Despite his apparent awareness of the subordination of women in society, he puts blame back on them, criticising his wife for her deceitfulness. Sam can recognise the restriction of women within society, but he does not consider that to be the problem so much as the treacherous nature – according to him – it produces in them.

After an argument with Bonnie about her ruined blouse, Henny borrows money from Ernie. The enterprising Ernie bargains for interest before 'dash[ing] upstairs' to 'make the addition to his accounts notebook' (p.61). In contrast, Sam 'had chimeric views about money' (p.62). This contrast enhances our sense of Sam's childishness and irresponsibility – his son has a more consistent and focused approach to financial matters than he does. Henny sees in her conscientious son her potential rescue from financial difficulties in the future, thinking, 'That boy will get me out of a mess later on' (p.62). Ironically, this prefigures her theft of his money later in the novel.

Q How does our view of the conflict between Henny and Sam evolve in this chapter?

Chapter Three (pp.69–92)

Summary: *Sam makes arrangements for his trip away, and Louisa visits a neighbour, Mrs Kydd, and kills a cat at her behest. Henny travels to town to see Bert Anderson.*

The section heading, 'Beautiful and childlike was he', refers to Sam, and further develops the reader's sense of his childishness. The pairing of 'beautiful' with 'childlike' suggests the desirability of Sam's uncomplicated nature, yet it is also ironic, given the frustration his attitude generates in those around him. While Sam sees himself as innocent and blissfully harmonised with the world, really he is blissfully ignorant.

Sam blames his family for limiting his achievements: 'It is a pity I had handicaps ... or I should have been able to accomplish all the wonderful things in my heart' (p.72). Again, Sam's ignorance is demonstrated through irony. While he complains about his own restriction, he restricts others, especially Henny, whose life has been hindered by bearing him numerous children, and by struggling to correct the family's dire financial situation with her own family's money. While Sam talks pompously of sacrifice, he is oblivious to the sacrifices others have made for him.

Sam's instructions to his sons for while he is away are telling of his sexism: 'I want you all to stand together and look after the house for me, not only the female hanni-miles [animals] ... but also the real honest-to-goodness hannimiles' (p.72). In grouping the women and the animals together, he is implying female subordination – both women and animals are to be protected and managed by men.

Louisa ventures beyond the world of her parents to visit the mysterious neighbour Mrs Kydd, whom Sam ridicules by calling 'Old Goat' (p.73). The reference plays on Mrs Kydd's surname (which sounds like 'kid', an infant goat), but it also implies childishness, since 'kid' is another word for a human child. Mrs Kydd is described as having a childlike face and 'chattering away like a little girl' (p.75). Mrs Kydd wants Louisa to kill a noisy cat, which she does. However, the unpleasant act does not earn Louie the appreciation she expects, and she feels manipulated: 'The old woman thanked her but rather perfunctorily' and 'bundled [her] out the front door' (pp.78, 79). Yet Louisa's desire to engage with Mrs Kydd suggests her fascination with women outside the house, and outside her father's approval.

Henny meets Bert Anderson, with whom she is having an affair, in a bar. She tells Bert of her misery and the family's financial difficulty. This allows readers to witness Henny's view of the Pollits' predicament and her disdain for her husband. She finds his rules oppressive – 'no cards, no dirty jokes, no drinks, no smokes, no lively books' (p.88) – but also feels that he is a hypocrite, embedding his less seemly interests in 'science': 'He lets that child of his read stuff about hysteria ... and animals breeding and old customs on European farms and all sorts of rot ... because it's science!' (p.88).

While Henny is open about her vices, Sam buries his in high-mindedness and 'dirty scientific books' (p.88). She also critiques his rhetoric of sacrifice, pointing out that the sacrifice is all hers: 'I'm the rich woman who can stop up all the holes' (p.89). Thus she highlights her husband's pretentiousness and double standards.

Q What does Henny's relationship with Bert Anderson offer each participant?

Chapter Four (pp.93–145)

Summary: *Sam's sister, Josephine, visits to reprimand her younger sister, Bonnie, for her affair with a married man. Sam's teasing of Louisa becomes venomous; Sam explains to Louisa his view of his marriage. Sam and Henny have an argument that culminates in violence.*

It is clear that Josephine possesses some of Sam's moralism when she arrives at the house to rebuke Bonnie: 'To think that a sister of mine should go out with a man like that, and a married man!' (p.95). However, her motives are ultimately selfish: 'I nearly died of shame ... Suppose they want to elect me to the chapter – and a rumor like that gets around?' (p.96). She also quickly switches from denouncing the affair to complaining about her income tax (p.98), indicating that her fervent concern is bundled up with her desire to be advantaged in life rather than genuine worry for her sister or others.

Sam's narcissism and sexist views are again on display when he states that he should not have to send his children to school: 'It's not even right they should be forced to go to school when they have a father like me: I can teach my children. I don't need schoolma'ams!' (p.109). He jocularly derides the idea that women should be among political representatives, as 'they is crazy!' (p.109). Ironically, he states that women 'need childer [children] to keep 'em from goin' crazy' (p.109); however, his wife has plenty of children and it has degraded her sanity and quality of life. Sam's comments indicate his strong views on women's 'proper' roles, and what he sees as the 'craziness' and ridiculousness of women in positions of influence.

The sympathy that Sam apparently feels for himself is not tempered with sympathy for others. When Sam thinks back to an earlier conversation with his friend Saul, the authorial tone is sarcastic, highlighting Sam's tendency towards martyrdom: 'Sam, like all men who have the traits of a man, had not failed to do, in the second year of marriage and ever since, what all real men do: he had confided his secret sorrow to a great many of his bosom friends' (p.118). The narration emphasises Sam's gossiping ('had not failed to do ... what all real men do') and his broadcasting of his apparently 'secret sorrow'. This phrasing underscores Sam's vain desire for others to admire his perseverance and sacrifice. Yet when Louisa, who has earlier been ridiculed by her father for her moodiness, tries to join the family in dancing to Bonnie's piano music, she is ridiculed for her appearance: 'Stop it, you fathead, you silly fathead' (p.113). Sam, in focusing on his daughter's looks, polices her attempt to move into the spotlight because she does not meet the physical standards he expects.

In conversation with Sam, Henny reveals that she doesn't want to talk to Louisa about menstruation and sex because she feels she will be ushering her into the miseries of womanhood: 'I couldn't drag her into all the muck of existence myself' (p.122). For Henny, Louisa's sexual maturation represents her crossing into the predatory, exploitative world Henny inhabits.

When Henny implies that Sam has had an affair, we see the latent violence behind Sam's purportedly 'righteous' persona surface. Louisa, in witnessing this, is further drawn into sympathy with Henny and disdain for her father: 'The look of concern she turned on her mother changed to rebuke when she looked at him' (p.125).

Q How does the language used by Stead on pages 117 and 118 influence our attitude towards Sam?

Chapter Five (pp.146–94)

Summary: *Louisa stays with the family of her deceased mother, the Bakens. After Henny collects her, they visit Henny's family at her estate, Monocacy. Henny converses with her mother and aunts, and it becomes clear that while Henny may be eccentric, the problems in her marriage are not unique.*

The largely wholesome family environment Louisa experiences at the Bakens' contrasts with the Pollit household. The Bakens' religiosity is foreign to Louisa, but she feels a sense of belonging (p.150). However, while his moody personality contrasts with Sam's cheerful disposition, Israel Baken, the grandfather, is another overbearing patriarch. The narrator also notes that 'All the Baken men had busy, discontented wives' (p.148), extending the novel's critique of marriage.

At Monocacy, Henny explains her feeling that there is no way for a woman to have a happy marriage:

> You fall madly in love with one man and nearly break your heart because he throws you over and years later you find out you would have been miserable with him; and you go with a man you don't care for and it's just the same with him too. (p.176)

Key point

This speaks to the novel's theme of inevitability or fate: Henny feels that life always manages to outmanoeuvre her and women generally. It also reinforces why she hasn't tried harder to make a break from Sam: she feels that life offers only constant defeat, and that the deck is always stacked against women.

The reader learns that Old David Collyer, Henny's father, effectively arranged the marriages of his daughters: he 'picked out Archie Lessinum and made him his clerk, then lawyer, then son-in-law, just as he had picked out Samuel Pollit and made him son-in-law and advanced him' (p.179). Marriage, in the world of the novel, is thus connected with financial advantage and reinforcing patriarchal power, rather than with love.

Q How does Louisa's stay with the Bakens in this chapter make her feel about her home? (Hint: read pages 155 and 156 closely.)

Chapter Six (pp.194–243)

Summary: *While in Malaya, Sam receives letters from his children, as well as from Gillian, the daughter of his colleague. He also has a falling-out with a colleague and suffers from the relentless heat.*

Louisa explains to the other children the Malay legend of 'Korinchi-men', wandering weretigers (men who transform into tigers) who seek to be admitted into a home before devouring the occupants. It is no coincidence that this story comes from Louisa (who is increasingly sceptical of patriarchal society): it may be read as a metaphor for the novel's predatory men. Like the Korinchi-man, Sam was born poor and thus is a sort of 'wanderer' who gains admittance to the Collyer family, but he progressively mismanages and devours his wife's finances and her spirit.

In discussion with his Indian colleague Naden (short for Abishengenaden), Sam, bizarrely, wishes he had a baby of every race, and states he is 'sorry that the kind of father I can be is limited' (p.210). This demonstrates his narcissism and need to exert his influence ubiquitously. The reality of white colonial power – the fact that men like him have already asserted themselves as metaphorical 'fathers' of colonised peoples – is lost on him.

For all his lofty sentiments, Sam is regarded as foolish. Naden observes that Sam speaks as one ignorant of the reality of colonial power and racial tension because, as a white man, he is unaffected by it: 'what can a white man in a country of white men know about anything of that sort?' (p.215). Noting that 'this is also a man who – Washington or no Washington – knows nothing about how his own country is run' (p.215), he reveals the hypocrisy in Sam's attitude: Sam is ignorant of political matters in his society even as he presumes to pontificate on racial and political tension in other nations.

As well as correspondence from his children, Sam receives a letter from Gillian Roebuck, a daughter of one of his colleagues. The letter has a somewhat formal tone and does not use sexual language, although its confessional nature suggests a secret and perhaps inappropriate relationship between Sam and Gillian. Gillian's age is not stated, although readers know from Sam's musings in Chapter One that he sees her as 'innocent' and a 'child-woman' (p.16). Thus the divisions between lover, teacher and father are uncomfortably blurred.

Sam writes a response to Gillian that continues to blur the boundaries between lover and father. He mentions that she is 'a young lady now' and so he can only call her 'My Little Gillian' before 'witnesses' (p.238), insinuating that he will regard her one way in public and another way in private. The sexual overtone is enhanced by Sam's mention of the heat, which provokes him to think about taking off his clothes: 'You just have one paramount thought, again conscious and subconscious, "Let's strip Jack naked!"' (pp.238–9). The letters add a sinister dimension to Sam's close relationship with the young woman.

Q On his trip, Sam speaks a great deal of his mind; what do his thoughts reveal about his character? How do others regard Sam and his views?

Chapter Seven (pp.244–306)

Summary: *Sam returns from Malaya, and an argument with the now-pregnant Henny breaks out. Sam's influence in the house has weakened, and his power outside the house is threatened by rumours that he refuses to address.*

The reader learns that while Sam was away in Malaya, 'in all the wild, vacant months that had passed, like a stupid, shouting, windy holiday', Sam's sons 'had never given one thought to their father's schemes and ideas' (p.247). Sam's influence in the house has waned, 'his wand broken' (p.247). Having been around adults so long, Sam has been deprived of the amplifying function of his children; whereas he used to construct himself as a kind of celebrity through them, magnifying his own power, upon his return he seems 'more restrained' (p.246). This reveals Sam's dependence on his children to maintain his jovial personality, but also suggests that the children are not as dependent on him as perhaps he would like to think.

Sam's Marxist ideals have been challenged by his exposure to the rewards of class hierarchy, such as porcelains and silks. While he attempts to reconcile his interest in 'the exquisite beauty, sensibility and sensuality of things treasured by those who put others in bondage' (p.266) with his socialist world view, the narrator's patronising tone – describing him as 'poor good man' (p.266) – suggests that he is deluded. Essentially, for all his high moral ideals, he too is seduced by the spoils of colonial power once he experiences them.

While Henny is upstairs, Sam and his father, Old Charles, agree that the child will be named after Charles, symbolising the perpetuation of patriarchy as a matter of power and tradition quite apart from any moral right or legitimacy. Earlier in the novel, Henny indicates resentment for Sam as the 'childnamer' (p.34), which is connected to his maintenance of power, and here we see that power being enacted again. While the labour of birth occurs outside of Sam's sight or experience, he will name the child as he pleases ('Charles-Franklin').

When accusations about Sam's behaviour at work are raised, he remains confident in his idealism and foolishly refuses to answer the charges. Despite his atheism, he uses religious language to suggest his trust in a greater power and his faith that the outcome will be favourable: 'There is a faith men live by; I have it in me' (p.304). This dogged faith is connected to his vanity. He mentions a motto Louisa has put up in her room – 'By my faith and hope I conjure thee, throw not away the hero in thy soul' (p.304) – and says 'she shows the power, the strength, and the glory of her poor Sam' (p.304). In reality, the motto strengthens Louie's independence *against* her father, yet Sam's narcissism leads him to interpret it flatteringly. Saul critiques Sam's confidence but admits 'when you talk you create a world' (p.305). Yet Sam's penchant for lofty oration really speaks to the strength of his delusion. He is so steadfast in his sense of moral righteousness that he will not even deign to address rumours against him, and yet he is so naive that he believes everything will be set right in the end.

Key point

As Sam's authority within the house weakens, his reputation outside of the house is also compromised, but he refuses to defend himself.

Q What does Sam's response to the rumours about him tell the reader about his personality?

Chapter Eight (pp.307–57)

Summary: *The family move to their new home, and Louisa falls in love with her teacher, Miss Aiden. Conflict intensifies between Sam and Louisa.*

Louisa initially makes fun of Miss Aiden, although she soon becomes fascinated by her. This demonstrates Louisa's desire for female connection and a female model of influence.

Sam is apprehensive of Louisa's burgeoning adolescence. The narration, adopting Sam's point of view, states, 'This was what her years of sullenness had concealed, not a quiet and patient nature, like her mother's, but a stern, selfish, vain nature like her grandfather's, wicked

Israel's angry seed' (p.322). He is terrified of her growing up, as he sees this as representing a threat to his control. More specifically, the reference to Louisa's deceased mother indicates his fear that his daughter does not fit the paragon of passive, domestic female virtue he believed his late wife to embody.

Louisa, who has been pushed to her limit and despairs about her future, asks Sam if she can move in with the Bakens. His response is typically controlling. Despite his sense of himself as a radical free-thinker, he rigidly enforces patriarchal tradition: 'a woman must not leave her father's home till she goes to her husband: that is what I am here for, to look after you' (p.356). He also blackmails her emotionally by insisting that it would make the conflict between himself and Henny worse: 'Do you want me to blame *her?*' (p.357) he asks, exploiting Louisa's concern for her stepmother. This episode clearly demonstrates Sam's manipulative nature and determination to prevent his daughter stepping outside his sphere of influence.

Key point

Conflict between Louisa and Sam grows, and Sam's domineering nature becomes more apparent in his attempts to stifle and control his daughter.

Q Why do you think Sam tries to convince Louisa that she needs to stay in the house?

Chapter Nine (pp.358–442)

Summary: *Henny makes a doll for her niece Cathy's eighteenth birthday; Louisa invites Miss Aiden to dinner; Sam continues to ignore Louisa's misery. Sam receives a letter telling him that he isn't the father of Charles-Franklin; Henny seeks to leave Sam, but Bert severs ties with her, leaving her stranded.*

Cathy's interest in dolls provides an interesting and symbolically rich reflection of women's position within patriarchal society. Because of her awkward appearance (described on page 358), Cathy is considered a challenging candidate for marriage; Aunt Hassie states harshly that 'men don't like wasp-waisted women anymore' (p.359). Cathy's interest in dolls is encouraged by her family, who believe that it will prepare her for motherhood by providing her with a nursery's worth of toys if she does ever get married. Meanwhile, it keeps her in a state of childhood till she can 'graduate' to womanhood through those roles. This reflects the lack of opportunities for women to pursue an identity beyond marriage and child-rearing. Furthermore, Henny's and Hattie's focus on the appearance of the dolls themselves is a sign of the emphasis placed on women's appearances (especially young women, such as Cathy and Louisa).

News that a local father has impregnated his teenage daughter provokes Sam's sense of moral outrage, but on behalf of the father instead of the daughter: 'Sam's hair rose on the first evening' and he was 'suddenly flaming with temper, shouting with rage' (p.371). Sam's urge to defend the father is too vehement. He sees the accusation as a generalised challenge to paternal authority, something he believes in strongly. More than this though, it evokes uncomfortably his quasi-sexual dominance of his daughter and his preference for vulnerable and childlike girls. Sam's passionate reaction is a symptom of his deep discomfort with and need to defend his own attitudes and behaviour. For Louie, the event seems to expose the evil of the world, 'an infernal middle kingdom of horror' (p.373).

As Louisa's hatred for Sam grows, so does her passion for Miss Aiden. However, when Miss Aiden visits, Sam dominates the conversation, again demonstrating his desire to maintain control and place himself at the centre of every interaction. Later, Sam receives an anonymous note informing him that he is not the father of his youngest child, leading Henny and Sam to argue. Henny seeks to leave Sam for Bert, but Bert ends their relationship, making a pretence of reforming his womanising ways. This leaves Henny without any help to escape her husband, and provides another instance of her exploitation.

Key point

Henny has resolved to leave Sam, only to have her avenue for escape cut off when Bert ends their affair. Meanwhile, Louie's antagonism towards her father increases. Both events build the sense of looming crisis in the lead-up to the novel's final chapter.

Q Why does news of the incestuous father amplify Louisa's feelings of dislike towards Sam?

Chapter Ten (pp.443–514)

Summary: *Bonny gives birth to a child, outraging Aunt Jo, and Sam collects a marlin and creates a family project of breaking it down into useful parts. Louisa plots to kill her parents, but only poisons Henny. She escapes the house forever.*

The all-pervading stink of the fish increases the feeling of suffocation and putrefaction in this family scenario that will soon reach its climax, as does the constant emphasis on 'boiling' in this section – the family tensions are also reaching their boiling point. Henny plays a game of patience, but keeps dealing fruitless hands, and the game quickly winds down: 'In five minutes the game was out! Henny forgot the storm and the fish in the copper and looked helplessly at the eight stacks of cards before her, each with a king on top' (p.461). The symbolism of the 'king on top' suggests the inevitable triumph of male dominance. Henny's hopelessness is reinforced by her feeling that the 'game she had played her whole life was finished' (p.461). With Bert, her only chance of escape, having recently left her, Henny is trapped and defeated; the game's conclusion foreshadows the conclusion of her life.

After Louisa sets out poisoned tea, which Henny chooses to drink, Louisa feels she has crossed a threshold, moving out of childhood forever: 'She was on the other side of a fence; there was a garden through the chinks that she had once been in, but could never be in again' (p.505). This speaks to the novel's theme of the loss of innocence (see 'Themes,

Ideas & Values'), which precipitates Louisa finally running away from the house for ever. As she moves further away, she thinks of her siblings: 'She pictured Ernie, Evie, the twins, darling Tommy' (p.514); however, she does not think of her father, indicating that she has at last achieved freedom from his influence.

Key point

Through her escape from the Pollit household, Louisa finally moves towards a destiny and identity beyond the influence of her father.

Q Has Henny changed from how she appears in Chapter Nine? If so, how?

CHARACTERS & RELATIONSHIPS

Louisa (Louie) Pollit

Key quotes

'If I didn't know I was a genius, I would die: why live?' (p.50)

'She was glowing with pleasure and imagining a harlequinade of scenes in which she, Louie, was acting, declaiming ... to a vast, shadowy audience stretching away into an opera house as large as the world, with tiers of boxes as high as the Cathedral at least.' (p.49)

'I have gone for a walk round the world.' (p.514)

Louisa is the eldest of the Pollit children – she is around twelve years old at the start of the novel. She is the child on whom the novel focuses most intensely and the character with whom we are most likely to identify. She is set apart from the other children by being the daughter of Sam and his first wife, Rachel, and thus Henny's stepdaughter. By the standards expected of her, Louisa is unattractive, overweight and clumsy, and Sam and Henny often use her size to ridicule her. This disdain from her father adds to her solitary and introverted nature; however, readers are granted access to her complex interior life. Louisa is sensitive, imaginative and highly artistic, and dreams of a future in which she can fulfil her potential. She feels trapped by her parents' endless rivalry and wishes they would kill each other to finally end the torment.

The night rider imagined or heard only by Louisa in the first chapter is symbolic of both her introversion and her particular level of awareness that surpasses the rest of her family: while everyone else is asleep, 'Louie and the rider on the red mare were wakers' (p.22). This moment also prefigures Louie's yearning for adventure beyond the house and her eventual escape at the end of the novel.

Artistic ambitions

Louisa devises poems, plays and stories throughout the novel, including an ambitious poetry cycle in honour of her teacher. Amid her chores, she fantasises about acting before a large audience, revealing her confidence in her intelligence and potential. Louie's artistic ability gives her self-belief despite her parents' put-downs, and she uses the negative experiences in her house to fuel her art (for instance, performing a play that echoes her father's treatment of her). Louie's dreams of fulfilling her potential are an important driver in her desire to escape the house and her expected role.

Relationship with Sam and Henny

Louisa's opposition to her father is central to the novel. Sam feels a sense of identification with his intellectual daughter but, much like his relationships with the other children, he wants her to internalise his views while remaining dependent on him. Sam is threatened by her adoption of other role models: when she develops a fascination with Miss Aiden, Sam makes sexist jokes about the teacher (p.65). He also often teases Louisa to maintain his superiority over her. Louisa is unique among the children in her ability to see through her father's happy-go-lucky persona to his need to dominate. His pet name for her, 'Looloo', contrasts with her increasingly introspective and adult identity.

The discomfort of Louisa's relationship to Sam is shown trenchantly when news circulates that a local father has gotten his daughter pregnant. Although Sam does not sexually abuse his daughter, the incident uncomfortably evokes the intrusive and manipulative closeness Sam fosters with his daughters, and Louisa begins to resent her father's power more thoroughly. Louisa tries various strategies of rebelling against Sam in order to get away from the family and her father's control; however, even when she confesses to plotting to kill Sam and Henny, he disregards her information and refuses to let her leave, selfishly using her as a 'bulwark' (p.468) against Henny's hatred.

Henny's behaviour is frequently outrageous and concerning, and she both verbally and physically abuses Louisa. However, Louisa is able to glimpse that her eccentric mother's words and actions are to a large extent a product of her treatment in her marriage and in society more broadly – that she is a woman frustrated and maddened by structures and expectations. Consequently, despite Louisa and Henny's apparent rivalry, the girl is able to form an understanding of Henny seemingly beyond that of other characters in the novel. Louisa's role in Henny's death (by putting the arsenic into a cup before Henny knowingly drinks it) is somewhat ironic given their strange closeness, and given that Louisa is the one who previously cared for Henny when she fainted.

Relationship with Miss Aiden

Louisa falls in love with Miss Aiden, her schoolteacher, and writes poems dedicated to her. Her attraction to Miss Aiden demonstrates her fascination with a figure beyond her manipulative father and men in general. She is captivated by this beautiful, intelligent woman who seems to indicate a world of possibility for women beyond the stifling structures of childhood under her father and the marital misery demonstrated by her parents.

Samuel (Sam) Pollit

Key quotes

'For Sam was naturally lighthearted, pleasant, all generous effusion and responsive emotion ... and tragedy itself could not worm its way by any means into his heart. Such a thing would have made him ill or mad, and he was all for health, sanity, success, and human love.' (p.45)

'Go and tell your father that if he wants to speak to me he can come downstairs to do it, even if he is the Great I-Am.' (p.119)

'"By Gemini," he thought, taking a great breath, "this is how men feel who take advantage of their power ... What it must be, though, to taste supreme power!"' (p.15)

Sam is the father and patriarch of the Pollit household, 'the man who loved children' after whom the novel is titled. Blond and attractive, he is thirty-eight at the start of the novel. He works as a conservationist and keeps various animals in cages at the family's first home. Sam is proud, playful and happy-go-lucky. However, his narcissism and self-confidence also cause him to ignore the emotional needs of his wife and children. He is self-centred and refuses to accept fault, using setbacks to emphasise what he sees as his courageous and sacrificial nature. In his marriage to Henny, Sam is self-righteous and proud: given his wife's volatility, he believes himself to be hard done by, and that he suffers his lot with infinite patience. However, in reality he ignores his wife's complaints, further marginalising her. Because of Sam's unwavering confidence in his own knowledge and moral authority, his character changes minimally throughout the novel.

Sam appears to love his children, but he places himself at the centre of their activities in a way that is ultimately domineering. He has grand, inflated nicknames for himself, such as 'Sam-I-Am' and 'Sam-the-Bold' (p.202) – names Henny ridicules by referring to him as 'the Great I-Am' and 'the Great Mouthpiece' (p.167). He uses his children as a receptive audience for his thoughts and theories on politics and philosophy. He also speaks to the children in a babyish made-up language, which emphasises not only the closed-off world he creates with them, but also his own childishness, and perhaps his desire to keep his children infantile. Like Peter Pan, Sam seems to hope he can never to grow up, and he uses his children to feed that illusion. When he returns from Malaya, Sam is described as having changed, likely because he has not had children as his audience; the removal of his childish followers seems to deprive him of some of his purpose.

Sam is highly sexist. He often comments on what he sees as the irrationality or inferiority of women, and he allocates the majority of housework to his female children. He teases Louisa for her weight and moodiness, indicating his expectations of female appearance and demeanour. He both encourages and stifles the ambitions of his talented eldest daughter; he encourages her to learn but makes himself the focus of her education, and refuses to allow her to leave the house until she marries. When Louisa discovers a female role model for herself (Miss Aiden), Sam attempts to degrade her view of the woman with crude jokes.

Henrietta (Henny) Pollit

Key quotes

'Look at me! My back's bent in two with the fruit of my womb; aren't you sorry to see what happened to me because of his lust?' (p.262)

'Henny was one of those women who secretly sympathize with all women against all men; life was a rotten deal, with men holding all the aces.' (p.34)

'You fall madly in love with one man and nearly break your heart because he throws you over and years later you find out you would have been miserable with him; and you go with a man you don't care for and it's just the same with him too.' (p.176)

Henny is Sam's second wife and mother of all the children except Louisa. Once elegant and 'glossy-eyed' (p.17), at the start of the novel she is thirty-six and worn down. Henny comes from a wealthy Baltimore family, but her family finances have been steadily depleted. In her marriage to Sam, she is eccentric and outrageous. She openly reviles her husband and her life in the Pollit house, and makes threats directed at both herself and her children, especially Louisa. Henny has feelings of contempt and disgust towards the world around her, but also great sympathy for those whom she sees as similarly downtrodden. She is deeply embittered by marriage and her experience of raising children, and feels that men are all alike in their exploitation of women as wives and baby-makers. She carries on an affair with a man, Bert Anderson, in Baltimore, and a rumour circulates that her youngest child, Charles-Franklin, is the result of this affair.

Henny and Sam's marriage is astonishingly bitter; they have not spoken regularly in years, and communicate in messages ferried by their children. Sam has positioned himself at head of the household, yet it is

Henny who tops up the finances with her family money as the household sinks further and further into debt. Sam seems to see his once-wealthy wife as a faded, corrupt aristocrat, whereas she sees her husband as a self-righteous hypocrite who oppresses her while pleading innocence. Henny resents Sam's condescending attitude and ignorance of the feelings of those around him. Nevertheless, she feels trapped in the relationship and even a sense of ownership over her own misery within it. This is represented in her relationship to the Pollit house:

> She had the calm of frequentation; she belonged to this house and it to her. Though she was a prisoner in it, she possessed it. She and it were her marriage. (p.5)

Stead thus indicates the connection of Henny's house and family to her own sense of identity and routine, even though this also fosters her resentment.

Despite her aggressive outbursts and threats, Henny fascinates the children, who see her as inhabiting a different world from that represented by her father. In her attitude to them, she alternates between impatience and indulgence. However, when Sam finds out about her affair, it becomes clear that she has an attachment to them that she is terrified Sam will sever.

Aunt Josephine

Key quotes

'To think a sister of mine should go out with a man like that, and a married man! You must stop it! I insist upon it, Samuel!' (p.95)

'Right is right, and wrong is wrong.' (p.96)

'I always do my duty. Some people don't like me for it, but I know why.' (p.97)

Aunt Jo is Sam's middle-aged sister, who owns a local boarding house. She is tall and assertive, and blue-eyed and blonde-haired like her brother. She also shares her brother's moral righteousness. However, in contrast to Sam, she is most concerned with her reputation.

In her first appearance in the novel (p.93), she arrives to berate Bonnie for an affair she has been having with a married man, scandalised that her sister could violate the institution of marriage. In expressing her disapproval, she uses the language of religious outrage; however, she seems mainly concerned about how the gossip will affect her own reputation.

The idea that Jo's investment in social appearances eclipses her concern for Bonnie's welfare is confirmed towards the end of the novel, when Bonnie turns up on her doorstep ready to give birth. Despite Bonnie's considerable distress, Jo is incensed at the compromising social position Bonnie has placed her in, worrying especially about damage to her business.

Minor characters

Bonnie Pollit

Key quote

> 'But Jo told her … that the horrible man went, straight from giving Bonnie a good time, to his wife's table and that everyone was talking and that there would be a frightful scandal.' (p.102)

Bonnie is Sam's younger sister. She is twenty-five years old and works as the Pollits' poorly paid maid. She is cheerful and often sings about the house as she works; but in Chapter Two Henny derides her for her promiscuity and messiness (pp.56–8). Bonnie respects Henny and treats her kindly, so she is upset by the harsh criticism, especially when she accidental burns Henny's blouse.

Bonnie carries on an affair with a married man, and thus becomes an object of scorn for her sister, Jo, who is obsessed with social appearances. Bonnie hopes that her lover will divorce his wife, but she agrees to terminate the affair when Jo tells her that the man and his wife are back together. However, later in the novel Bonnie has fallen pregnant to the same man. The ease with which she is taken advantage of suggests that she has not yet developed the cynicism about men that characterises Henny and her sisters.

Ernest (Ernie) Pollit

Key quote

'He was a charming child, everyone's darling, he made no enemies, and he managed to remain above the domestic battle through concentration on his money matters.' (p.61)

Ernest, one of the Pollit children, is well liked within the family. The Pollits' difficulties with money have given Ernie an interest in financial matters (unlike his father), and his focus on money helps to distract him from the miseries of the household. He is skilled in accountancy for his age, and Henny privately hopes he will save her from poverty when he grows up. While Sam engages his children to work without payment, Henny pays Ernie for his work, teaching him a more practical and realistic approach to money. Ironically, while Henny and Ernie's closeness is predicated on his financial acumen, she steals his savings before she dies, distressing her son and deeply damaging their relationship.

Evie Pollit

Key quote

'She had many petnames, any, in fact, that occurred to Sam, such as Penthestes (a chickadee) or Troglodytes (the house wren), names of engaging little dusky birds or animals.' (p.24)

Of his children, Sam is most confident of the adoration of Evie. The pet name 'Little Womey' (his 'Little Woman') indicates Sam's tendency to use his daughters as emotional replacements for his wife, while still infantilising them. It also foreshadows events late in the novel; when Louisa, who provides the majority of maternal care for the other children, rejects her father, Evie is picked out as his new favourite.

Bert Anderson

Key quote

> 'This red-cheeked, lusty, riotous giant was not a gentleman, but he treated [Henny] as a single girl.' (p.86)

Bert, Henny's 'stand-by from the Department of Internal Revenue' (p.86), is the man with whom Henny is having an affair. In contrast to Sam, with his lofty ideals, Bert is focused on more immediate gratification. He is 'red-cheeked, lusty, riotous' (p.86). Whereas Sam is fascinated by politics and has a stringent sense of morality, Bert does not bother himself with deep thought on these topics. Henny likes him because, unlike Sam, whose voice is always central in any conversation, Bert listens to her and is enthused by her presence.

However, Bert loses interest in Henny as her financial struggles become more apparent. While Sam foolishly hangs on to his relationship with Henny through all kinds of obstacles despite the misery it generates, Bert leaves her as soon as knowledge of the affair threatens to get out; he cannot provide Henny with any assistance and fears for his reputation.

Saul Pilgrim

Key quote

> 'He admired Sam for his glorious, messianic belief in himself ... but now he felt impelled to tell Sam some of the truths of life.' (p.304)

Saul Pilgrim is an old friend of Sam's. For the last seventeen years he has written a serialised story for a magazine that he has never been able to bring to a conclusion. This desire for 'the problem to resolve itself accidentally' (p.304) seems to reflect the narrative of the Pollit marriage, which similarly proceeds dramatically yet without purpose. When slanderous rumours begin circulating about Sam, Saul urges his friend to answer the charges against him and set the record straight, but is unsuccessful in persuading the idealistic Sam.

Aunt Hassie

Key quote

'Henny got on well with Hassie, had a lot of fun with her, and collaborated with her.' (p.359)

Hassie Collyer, Henny's sister, lives in Baltimore and is a support for Henny, often lending her money and taking her shopping. Hassie is the mother of Cathy, whom she derides for her weight and her awkward figure, which she believes will make it difficult for Cathy to find a man to marry.

Cathy Collyer

Key quote

'Her face was oval and empty of all but a little child's experience.' (p.358)

Cathy is the only child of Aunt Hassie, Henny's sister. She is eighteen years old, unattractive by the standards of the world around her and deeply self-conscious about her figure, thanks partly to Hassie's proclamations on what men want in a woman. Cathy is passionate about dolls, owing to a childhood without other companions, and this fascination is encouraged by her mother. Hassie feels that if her plain daughter never marries, she will at least have her extensive doll collection to keep her occupied; and if she does, the collection can be passed down to her children. Cathy's relationship to the dolls demonstrates the limited roles available for women in the world of the novel.

The Collyer family

Key quote

Henny to Sam: 'Where would you be without the Collyer style? … You don't know where your bread and butter comes from.' (p.137)

The rest of the Collyer family appears in the novel infrequently. David Collyer is patriarch of the once-rich Baltimore family from which Henny comes, and was head of a prosperous seafood business. He is the original owner of Tohoga House, the Pollits' first home, and provides them with financial help. He dies during the course of the novel (in Chapter Seven), escalating the Collyers' and Pollits' descent into poverty.

'Old Ellen' Collyer is Henny's mother, who lives in the family's house, Monocacy, which has fallen into disrepair as the family's finances have declined. She is fiery and irreverent and does not moderate her speech around the children. Ellen listens to Henny's startling and dramatic complaints about Sam (which include her contemplations of suicide). She shares her daughter's marital frustrations, thereby indicating the multi-generational nature of female dissatisfaction with marriage.

Norman Collyer is Henny's eldest brother. He sends her a letter at the start of the novel, withholding money. He seems to harbour some resentment towards Henny, since he refers to her as having been 'Father's pet' (p.12). He assumes that the mess Henny's family are in is her fault (rather than her husband's), demonstrating the pervasive sexism of the world of the text.

Uncle Barry is Henny's other brother, who lives with her mother, Old Ellen. He is charming, but drinks and womanises. Ultimately, he presents as another presumptuous male; for instance, Ellen describes how he grabbed her behind after mistaking her for the washerwoman.

Miss Aiden

Key quote

> 'Louie had formed a magnificent project, the Aiden Cycle. The Aiden Cycle would consist of a poem of every conceivable form and also every conceivable meter ... each and every one ... in honour of Miss Aiden.' (p.332)

Miss Aiden is the attractive young teacher whom Louisa comes to adore, and who eventually visits the house for dinner. Miss Aiden is an important indicator of Louisa's interests outside of the family home, and outside the male-defined world of her father.

Clare Meredith

Key quote

'Her appetites were excited by a classmate named Clare ... a tall, vigorous, yellow-haired girl with boy's curls and a splendid medallion face.' (p.331)

Clare is a jokey and outrageous schoolfriend of Louisa's who lives in the same area. Clare is poor, often attending school in decaying clothes, and pitied by her teachers. She makes light of her situation, even auctioning off items of clothing as soon as she arrives at school. However, Clare's humour around her poverty conceals a sense of hopelessness that she will never escape it. She is Louie's first real friend outside of her family; however, Sam characteristically intrudes into the relationship, visiting Clare with Louie unannounced.

Rachel Pollit

Key quote

'... dear Rachel, the great love ...' (p.133)

Rachel was Sam's first wife, and the mother of Louisa. She died several years before the novel opens, but Sam speaks of her in glowing and idealistic terms. However, while Sam considered her a perfect wife, late in the novel the contents of a letter reveal that she did not consider him a perfect husband, and did not think he understood women or children.

Hazel Moore

Key quote

'When I see what you've been through with that man and his parcel of children, Henny, I think I'm better off.' (p.193)

Hazel is Henny's former housekeeper and one of her few friends. She is middle-aged and has been engaged to a younger man for the last fifteen years. Henny wishes to employ Hazel while Sam is in Malaya, but Sam is against the idea, partly because of Hazel's religiosity. Hazel's priest will not permit her to marry her lover until she is too old for children because her partner is Protestant and the priest does not wish her to have

Protestant children. This absurd scenario provides another example of social forces conspiring against women's autonomy.

Abishengenaden (Naden)

Key quote

'His affection for Sam was temporary and had something patronizing in it.' (p.214)

Sam's Indian clerk during the Malaya trip is aware of social hierarchies; he is a bureaucrat and thus sees himself as 'higher' than many of those around him. Serious in nature, he is polite and deferential to Sam, but regards him as ignorant and somewhat ridiculous.

THEMES, IDEAS & VALUES

Gender roles and sexism

Key quotes

'Look at me! My back's bent in two with the fruit of my womb; aren't you sorry to see what happened to me because of his lust?' (Henny, p.262)

'En if I had my way no crazy shemales would so much as git the vote! Becaze why? Becaze they is crazy! Becaze they know nuffin! Becaze if they ain't got childer, they need childer to keep 'em from goin' crazy; en if they have childer the childer drive em crazy.' (Sam, p.109)

'... life was a rotten deal, with men holding all the aces.' (p.34)

The limited roles and diminished power available to women in a patriarchal society is an important theme in *The Man Who Loved Children*. The novel is filled with empowered men and powerless women. For example, it is rumoured that Louisa's neighbour, Mrs Kydd, is beaten by her husband. Bonnie is having an affair with a man who will not leave his wife, and Henny's lover, Bert, abandons her once news of the affair breaks.

Within the Pollit home, Sam is deeply sexist and has a clear and prescribed sense of gender roles, exploiting his female children, especially through housework. While Sam has many idealised visions of political harmony, his view of a 'brotherhood of man' (p.47) makes no mention of women, effectively excluding at least half of humankind from his utopia. Henny also makes clear her resentment of Sam's exploitation of her as a mere baby-maker, feeling forced to have child after child – children Sam uses to feed his pride and ego. Henny and Sam should have equal right as parents, yet Sam, as the male, assumes he is head of the household, treating it as a private kingdom. Henny feels that life with her husband has wasted her, and that she does not even have much influence over her children in the narrow domestic sphere to which she is virtually confined.

As Louisa ages, and her curiosity, intelligence and ambition develop, she suffers considerably under her father's (and society's) expectations of her gender. She is exploited and asked to do more than her fair share of housework, but when she rebels against her father, he derides her appearance, reminding her of her failure to reach his standards of female worth. Similarly, Louisa's fascination with her clever and charming teacher, Miss Aiden, is threatening to her father, not only because as a vain patriarch he wants to be the focus of attention himself, but also because his view of women's prescribed roles is so narrow.

Aunt Hassie's only child, Cathy, is another example of a woman suffering under her prescribed role. The text makes clear that Cathy is physically undesirable, judged by the standards of the day. Consequently, Cathy is 'deeply ashamed of her figure' and 'stooped to hide it' (p.359). Her mother encourages Cathy's childhood enthusiasm for dolls well into her teenage years. This provides a way of keeping Cathy stalled in childhood because, in the world of the novel, she does not have the traits required to transition into adulthood by serving as a wife and mother. Moreover, Hassie feels that if Cathy gets married, the dolls will come in handy for her own children, automatically assuming that Cathy will have babies, and that Cathy's daughters will be locked into the same tradition. Examples like this are indicative of the novel's depiction of a culture in which women endure roles ultimately traceable to male desires and interests.

Key point

The novel depicts a world in which the roles of women are frustratingly narrow, and through which many women come to grief.

An important aspect of Louisa's character is her ability to understand the ways in which women are oppressed, and to have ambitions beyond those boundaries. In Chapter Two, Sam makes Louisa recite quotations of thinkers he admires – who are all men, of course. He suggests tokenistically that one of the inspirational sayings might apply to women too, yet Louisa cleverly insinuates that it does not, because women are denied the same opportunities as men (p.41). Louisa is aware of the deep social and historical forces that push against women's equality and independence. She dreams of being a great artist, and shows considerable artistic enthusiasm and talent for her age, but knows she must escape the house if she is ever to fulfil her potential.

Male narcissism

Key quotes

'You will never understand, Looloo-dirl, what I suffered: but I have battled my way through. Fate puts stones in the path of those she wants to try; she found I had stuffing in me and is satisfied.' (Sam, p.127)

'It's not even right they should be forced to go to school when they have a father like me: I can teach my children. I don't need schoolma'ams!' (Sam, p.109)

'Perhaps he, Samuel Clemens Pollit, was a forerunner of the truly great man.' (p.15)

The novel is dominated by Sam's tremendous narcissism and sense of entitlement. He uses his children as an audience for his ideas, desiring to have his own sense of greatness reflected back at him.

Sam's pseudo-intellectualism and idealism, combined with his ignorance of the feelings of those around him, is central to Henny's resentment of him. Moreover, although Sam is especially deluded and self-absorbed, the novel suggests that this is a broader feature of the male-dominated society in which the novel is set. When Henny and the children visit Monocacy, for instance, the women there each complain about the self-important and lazy men in their lives.

As befits his narcissism, Sam sees the strife within his family only through the lens of his own importance. When he speaks to his daughter about his disastrous marriage, he frames it as a 'test' of his virtue or stamina: 'Fate puts stones in the path of those she wants to try; she found I had stuffing in me and is satisfied' (p.127). Instead of acknowledging his and Henny's deep incompatibility and the misery they bring on each other, he vainly interprets the marriage as a test from above to allow him to prove himself through suffering. Despite his atheism, Sam sees himself as a

Christ-like figure, and this inflated sense of himself allows everything to be about him. Even after his wife's suicide, rather than reassess his life in light of her misery, Sam uses the event to further inflate the sense of virtue and honour he projects. Henny died owing a considerable amount of money, and Sam resolves to pay her debts off gradually – not out of any true sense of duty, but as a way of trumpeting his own noble nature (pp.501–2).

Sam's narcissism is obviously damaging to many other characters in the novel, especially Henny and Louisa. However, it also aids in his own declining fortunes. When his job is threatened, he clings to a sense that his virtue will shine through and his opponents will be defeated; he is completely convinced that his view of the world will prevail. He also fails to realise that his position did not stem from his own inherent merit; actually, he owes his career to the influence of Henny's father and, consequently, when Henny's father isn't there to protect him, he is vulnerable to his opponents.

Key point

Sam's confidence in his own importance and the correctness of his ideas makes him dismissive or ignorant of contrasting views.

National paternalism

Key quotes

'Think of the logcutters' children in Oregon and the little redskins on Indian reservations and the little tall-eared Missourians and the little frozen two-legged ears of Minnesota Swedish wheat whose only dream in life is to come and see the Great White Father …' (Sam, pp.70–1)

'I wish I had a black baby too. A tan one, a Chinese one – every kind of baby. I am sorry that the kind of father I can be is limited.' (Sam, p.210)

'"You are but an ebonized Aryan, Naden, and I am the bleached one that is fashionable at present." Naden pretended not to hear this.' (Sam, p.215)

Through several episodes, most obviously the visit to Monocacy, Stead's novel makes clear that Sam's faults are shared by other men, implicating a culture in which men are convinced of their own superiority in emotional, intellectual and moral terms. This critique extends to national attitudes: Sam is also depicted as a reflection of an American 'paternal' attitude to social progress and other peoples and nations. He doesn't only represent one man knowing what's good for everyone else, but also a national ethos of assumed superiority.

Sam is positioned as representative of stereotypical white, middle-class American values; he believes in the American Dream – an idealised vision of opportunity for freedom and success – while ignoring the real struggles of others. For example, he tells his own children that the 'only dream in life' of children from various ethnic backgrounds 'is to come and see the Great White Father – whomever he may happen to be' (p.71), constructing white middle-class values as the implicit aim of all cultures. After Sam loses his job at the Conservation Department, he starts a radio program using the persona 'Uncle Sam' (p.508) – explicitly linking himself with the personification of the United States. Sam's ideals focus on nationalistic folktales and praise for American freedom and values, in comparison with 'poor bonded Europe' (p.506). This nationalistic celebration ignores the various subordinate groups within the novel about which Sam is unaware, especially women. Sam idolises many Americans of historic significance, yet his adulation is superficial and self-aggrandising, and feeds a world view that is simplistic and inattentive to context and differences.

Key point

Sam's self-righteousness and tendency to position himself as a secular saviour is also representative of dominant national values.

Sam's role as a representative of American cultural and moral imperialism is perhaps most clear in the passages set in Malaya. In this section, Sam's intolerance of the heat, which he finds relentless and oppressive, symbolises his inexperience with realities beyond his own. In Malaya, Sam espouses many of his grand theories of power and political organisation. Yet he is oblivious to the power struggles going on within the country between different races and classes. While his expedition is intended to be one of discovery, the chapter serves to demonstrate Sam's cluelessness, and he is regarded by others as naive and foolish. When he comments freely on racial issues affecting the region, his guide, Naden, thinks, 'what can a white man in a country of white men know about anything of that sort?' (p.215). In this episode especially, Sam functions as a symbol of a general American idealism and ignorance. Moreover, upon his return, the reader learns that he has acquired various exotic possessions from the country, thus repeating the gestures of colonial power.

Language and power

Key quotes

'"Sam," said Saul fervently, "when you talk, you know you create a world."' (p.305)

'After this striking scene in double-dutch, Sam, looking pale with annoyance, asked what the Devil was the use of writing in Choctaw. What language was it? Why couldn't it be in English?' (p.394)

'The Aiden Cycle would consist of a poem of every conceivable form and also every conceivable meter ... every one ... in honour of Miss Aiden.' (p.332)

The language used by several characters in *The Man Who Loved Children* is distinctive, and holds important thematic implications for those characters and the novel as a whole. At the start of the novel, Henny and Sam have not been speaking but communicating by relaying messages between the children, implying that speech is a significant indicator of acknowledgement and respect that is presently being denied. When they speak to the children, it becomes clear through Henny's and Sam's differing language that they have fundamentally different world views.

Sam uses language as a tool of his power and self-perception. His high-flown speech suggests his own grandeur and moral superiority, while he uses deliberately babyish language to disconnect from the adult world and infantilise others. He cultivates a collection of 'pet' names for his family members, as well as insulting names for neighbours he dislikes, reinforcing his sense of power and ability to define the world around him. Yet Sam also deludes himself with his language. His friend Saul comments that when Sam speaks he is able to 'create a world' (p.305), but that 'world' is an evasion that prevents Sam from addressing the reality that his job and reputation will slip away. Similarly, in Malaya, Naden, who listens to Sam espouse his theories, sees him as one who, for all his lofty talk, has little idea of others' reality. For Sam, language is a tool of power, but also of ignorance.

Henny's use of language throughout the novel contrasts starkly with Sam's, and is an important aspect in revealing her world view. In the first chapter she describes those she has seen in town through a rush of grotesque descriptions that combine animality, physical disgust and sexual imposition (pp.6–8). Her choice of descriptors works to mark her as one who sees the world as pitiful, obscene and intrusive – and, crucially, this is reflective of her experience and the result of her feelings of despair and degradation. Animal imagery is used to reflect base desires – sex, power, violence, self-interest – and she also applies them to her husband, 'a brute, a savage, a wild Indian' whose love is 'beastly' (p.139). Henny's distinctively volatile speech marks her as one in perpetual revolt against the power Sam represents. The colourful, derogatory language she uses is expressive of her frustration.

Language is also intertwined with power for the sensitive and poetic (yet largely silent) Louisa. Louisa is a prolific producer of words, keeping a diary, as well as producing a cycle of poems dedicated to her teacher. For Louisa, this production of language is linked to her own artistic potential and individuality. However, her language (both of complaint and of artistry) is consistently ridiculed or disregarded by her father. Eventually, however, Louisa uses language to confront Sam when she performs a play in a language that he cannot understand. Whereas Sam has previously asserted dominance over the family through language, Louisa positions herself as a creator, greatly annoying her father and challenging his dominance.

Key point

Language can be used to manipulate and define the world for one's own benefit, and at the expense of others; however, language also forms an important means by which power can be contested.

Loss of innocence

Key quotes

'... the noises, cries, philosophies of others seemed like silly games that kindergarten children play. She was on the other side of a fence; there was a garden through the chinks that she had once been in, but could never be in again.' (p.505)

'MEGARA: ... As mother says, I am rotten: but with innocence.' (p.394)

The theme of innocence is significant to Stead's novel in at least two ways. Crucially, the text focuses on Louisa's growing up and her accompanying feelings of losing her innocence. At the start of the novel, we learn that the introspective Louisa feels agitated when her parents are around. Whereas the younger children regard their parents as opposing gods, and are oblivious to the intensity of the antagonism because they do not understand it, Louisa is on the cusp of the adult world herself. As she matures, she comes to realise the nature of the conflict between her parents – to grasp the power dynamic between them and to sympathise with Henny's bitter resentment of her role.

Unlike the other children, Louisa is also able to see through her father. Whereas children commonly perceive their parents as figures of moral authority and virtue, part of growing up is embracing a more complicated and often critical perspective. Louisa's parents are, of course, far from ideal, and the novel partly illustrates her shifting attitude to them and her questioning, rebellion and resentment that stems from that.

Louisa's attempt to kill her parents draws a permanent line between her childhood and adulthood. In taking control of a situation so dramatically, she renounces the role of long-suffering and ultimately dutiful daughter. The novel's conclusion sees her decision to leave the house, probably forever, in order to become a whole person, and not one either confined to the unknowing realm of childhood or painfully fused to the oppressive and subordinate role Sam has outlined for her. Sam wishes his children to remain innocent and subordinate; in Louisa's rejection of this and her eventual escape, Stead constructs the loss of innocence – the abandoning of this expected identity – as necessary for liberation.

In contrast to Louisa, Sam spends the novel playing at a kind of innocence that seems to belie his true nature and power. He claims to be bewildered by the cause of Henny's hostility towards him, as well as his daughter's resentment. In his games about the home, he affects a childish persona that exempts him from the very adult power he actually exerts. Sam plays at being a Peter Pan–like figure so he can remain the adored leader, maintaining his sense of his own specialness. Whereas Louisa sees innocence as a role trapping her, Sam presents himself as an 'innocent' to maintain his power.

Culpability and blame

Key quotes

'After a pause he said gloomily, "Even at that I am not sure she did not want to commit actual crimes."' (Sam, p.129)

'"Any marriage I made would have gone smash," cried Henny, scoffing and throwing back her head: "I was born for excitement."' (p.434)

We are often accustomed to fiction in which we are encouraged to identify with 'likeable' key characters and reject other characters, who may be marked out as 'villains', and whom we can single out for blame. *The Man Who Loved Children* depicts a household stalled perpetually in misery, a misery that is only amplified throughout the course of the book. Who is the cause of all of this? Sam certainly seems to attract the most blame in *The Man Who Loved Children*. He may be affable and good-natured, but he is also egotistical; he is convinced of his own superiority and reacts in abusive ways when challenged.

Yet Stead's depiction of his rival, Henny, is far from idealistic, and suggests that she is not entirely without fault. Much of Henny's misery can be traced to the way her husband treats her; while she was once a wealthy society girl, she feels worn down by male-dominated society generally and marriage specifically. Yet she is also alarmingly violent towards Louisa, and threatens to kill both herself and her stepdaughter, clearly perpetrating abuse of her own. On page 129, Sam seems genuinely concerned that Henny might actually have harmed Louisa. Moreover, towards the end of the novel Henny suggests that any marriage she was in would have been a disaster – that she was 'born for excitement' (p.434). This suggests that Sam is not uniquely at fault for the state of the Pollit household, and reflects the complexity of assigning blame in such circumstances.

The question of culpability or blame becomes more pointedly relevant in the final chapter, when Henny and Louisa effectively collude to bring about Henny's sudden death. Louisa plans to kill both parents, but fumbles at the last moment, feeling sudden regret. Henny, understanding Louisa's intention, drinks the tea herself. This might absolve Louisa of the crime, since Henny drank the tea knowingly. However, despite having threatened suicide for years, Henny may not have done this if her stepdaughter hadn't prepared the situation for her. You might like to consider whose fault you feel this event is. Is it Sam and the oppressive society he represents, which have driven Henny and Louisa to despair? Is it Louisa, for taking an unacceptably dramatic approach to her situation – indeed, one too much befitting the literary myths she reads and writes? Is it Henny's fault, since she actively chooses the poison? Or is it a combination of all of these?

Key point

The messiness of life means that it is often difficult to limit blame to a single character or action.

Inevitability

Key quotes

'[Louisa] still believed that she had done the only right thing, the only thing ... Fate itself had not only justified her but saved her from consequences.' (p.505)

'Henny ... looked helplessly at the eight stacks of cards before her, each with a king on top. The game that she had played all her life was finished; she had no more to do; she had no game.' (p.461)

There is an intriguing theme of inevitability, or fate, running through Stead's novel that further complicates the notion of blame. As the text builds to its climax, Henny is playing a game of patience – a game of chance. The first hand she deals is impossible to work with; the second is unsatisfyingly easy, and Henny finishes the ordinarily protracted game quickly.

Being either impossible or dissatisfying, the card games symbolise Henny's trapped position and that the end is near for her as a character: 'The game she had played all her life was finished; she had no more to do; she had no game' (p.461). Henny reshuffles and begins to play again, but is struck by the game's pointlessness. Henny is trapped by her attachment to the children, and her attempts to leave Sam have been thwarted; there is nothing left for her except, presumably, a life of further skirmishes and misery with her ignorant husband. Hence at the end of the game the 'king' is still 'on top' (p.461).

Louisa also connects the idea of fate or inevitability to Henny's death. Her plan to murder both parents seems to fall through when she panics preparing the tea. However, Henny intuits that Louisa has poisoned the cup, and drinks anyway, carrying the plan (at least partly) to fruition as if it were inevitable. Afterward, Louisa, while scared, does not regret the decision, seeing it as fated: 'Fate itself had not only justified her but saved her from consequences' (p.505). It irritates Louisa to hear her father mention his wife's 'dreadful deed' (p.505), no doubt because of Sam's refusal to acknowledge any culpability, but also because she sees Henny's death as inevitable rather than an aberration. Thus, the theme of an inevitable 'destination' to the story – something tragic but inescapable – is woven throughout Stead's novel.

DIFFERENT INTERPRETATIONS

Different interpretations arise from different responses to a text. Over time, a text will evoke a wide range of responses from its readers, who may come from various social or cultural groups and live in very different places and historical periods. Responses by critics and reviewers can be published in newspapers, journals and books, both online and in print. They can also be expressed in discussions among readers in the media, classrooms and book groups.

While there is no single correct reading or interpretation of a text, it is important to understand that an interpretation is more than a personal opinion – it is the justification of a point of view on the text. To present an interpretation of a text based on your point of view, you must use a logical argument and support it with relevant evidence from the text.

Critical viewpoints

Critical reception of *The Man Who Loved Children* was minimal on the novel's initial release. It commanded some, but ultimately little, attention in the United States, and less in England. *The Man Who Loved Children* was an unconventional book, challenging in its style and content, and several early reviewers struggled to know how to approach it. Early reviews focused on the novel as a study of the middle-class family, noting the personalities and power dynamics central to the Pollit home. Thus, they tended to disregard the text's wider political implications, such as its searing critique of gender roles.

It was following the novel's republication in 1965 that critical attention and appraisal became more concerted. In this period, the contribution of women writers to the Australian literary tradition was attracting interest, especially as feminism's cultural and intellectual influence increased. Consequently, when the novel re-emerged, its portraits of gender relations seemed, to contemporary critics, clearer and more pressing (indeed, feminist critique has continued to feature significantly in discussion of Stead's novel). Critical interpretations of *The Man Who Loved Children* have not clashed significantly over the novel's key themes, and analyses largely work to complement one another. Nevertheless, critics and scholars have focused on exploring a range of significant features.

Shirley Walker (2000) focuses on language and notions of the 'artistic' in Stead's novel. She cites language as a deep indicator of characters' natures and world views, especially in relation to Henny and Sam. She points out that Henny's language relies heavily on animal metaphors, making it 'grossly physical and sexually predatory' (p.117), but also that Henny's language indicates that she 'sees life always in the same patterns of victimisation and oppression' (p.120). Sam's language, she suggests, is morally and philosophically high-sounding but ultimately empty and self-serving; it indicates that Sam is a character who, for all his supposed wisdom, has lost touch with reality. Walker's discussion of Louisa emphasises 'the growth of an artist in a hostile family environment' (p.127), and contrasts her with her father, Sam. Walker suggests that with his numerous improvised (but formulaic) songs and poems, Sam strives – but fails – to be an artist, descending into cliché. Consequently, Sam is challenged by the true artistic spirit of his daughter, who is able to process her degrading and difficult experiences into creative power and momentum.

Judith Kegan Gardiner focuses instead on the conflict between Louisa and Sam. For her, Stead highlights the ridiculousness of Sam's delusions of his own importance and 'champions the female rebel' (Gardiner 2000, p.146), Louisa, who undermines his power. This line of analysis might provoke the question of how much we as readers align ourselves with Louisa and accept her actions towards the end of the novel – specifically her role in Henny's death.

Two interpretations

Interpretation 1: Sam is ultimately to blame for the novel's tragic events.

The novel devotes considerable space to depicting Sam's personality and its effect on his family. Sam is arrogant and egotistic, certain of the accuracy and moral superiority of his own world view. This means he is either ignorant of the suffering around him, or he reinterprets it as a 'test' of his character (p.127), virtually ensuring that the suffering will continue. Sam seeks unity within his family, yet without trying to actually mend anything or understand the true nature of his wife's dissatisfaction. For example, early in the novel he simply demands that the 'everlasting schism' between himself and Henny must cease (p.43). After he discovers Henny's affair, rather than allow her a divorce, Sam perpetuates the family's misery by using his knowledge of her affair to amplify his power, threatening to take the children away. Henny's disdain and despair stems from her husband's selfish and domineering attitude, creating immense tension in the house. Therefore, it is ultimately Sam who forces the situation to boiling point, culminating in Henny's suicide.

Louisa, of course, is also instrumental in her stepmother's death – but she is pushed to the limit by her father too. Sam teases and belittles his daughter, attempting to crush her into a conformity that involves her taking after him. Louisa challenges Sam at several points and strongly desires to exert her independence, but Sam consistently ignores her complaints (e.g. pp.396–7), ensuring her continued entrapment and misery. Louisa's attempt to kill her parents does not arise from any innate 'badness' but is clearly the result of years of agonising domestic life from which Sam simply will not let her escape.

Sam's domination is not 'unconscious' or 'unintentional' in a way that absolves him of blame. On page 471, Sam appeals with passion to Louisa, sobbing over his wife's affair and insisting that Louisa stay with him because he has 'had too many burdens'. However, after he assumes her silence signifies agreement, he goes 'cheerfully back' to poking the fire. This sudden shift of emotion reveals Sam's manipulative nature: he gives a performance of feeling wounded in order to get what he wants.

Stead's text is strewn with numerous references to Sam's damaging egotism. The moral virtue he espouses and ostensibly presents is undoubtedly intended to contrast with the misery he generates around him. Despite his atheism, Sam aspires to the power of a god over his private world of 'Pollitry' and must therefore be considered the cause of the novel's tragic events.

Interpretation 2: Sam has a share in the misery of the novel's events, but they are ultimately traceable to broader forces beyond him.

Sam is foolish and often mean-spirited throughout the novel, but Stead is also careful to not merely demonise him. Sam is not a rogue egotist, but part of the oppressively sexist culture in which he lives. The novel is filled with women who have been victimised by entitled men. Uncle Barry's mistress threatens suicide because he won't marry her (p.160); Bonnie is seeing a man who will not leave his wife for her (p.101); and Mrs Kydd is beaten by her husband (p.76). After Henny tries to arrange to leave Sam, Bert tells her he will meet her at a bar after work, but instead he abandons her (p.442). Even Henny laments that her husband isn't anything 'special' in terms of his oppressiveness: 'all men are the same' (p.446). Therefore, while Sam is certainly an oppressive force within the novel, blame cannot stop with him and instead must be traced outward to the oppressive culture of which he is a product.

Furthermore, despite benefiting from sexism, Sam is actually depicted as unaware of his power and the damage it causes, and thus to some extent 'innocent'. There are several suggestions of his innocence or naivety. These are most prominent in his obsession with being the leader of his gang of children; the narrator tells us, 'All the children … believed that Sam was utterly innocent, which in fact he was, innocent too, of all knowledge of men, business, and politics, a confiding and sheltered child strayed into public affairs' (p.327). This complicates the idea that

Sam is singularly culpable for the Pollits' worsening situation, as he is actually too emotionally imperceptive to realise the error of his ways.

Another key reason to broaden the scope of blame in the novel is Henny's characterisation. Henny is volatile and sometimes violent, directing threats at both her husband and herself. This volatility is demonstrated at numerous points throughout the novel. While it might be tempting to read her character as purely a symptom of her husband's emotional abuse, Henny herself admits that 'Any marriage I made would have gone smash … I was born for excitement' (p.434). Ultimately, the events of the novel cannot be singularly or simplistically reduced to the work of one character; Stead constructs a world of oppressive forces and unusual personalities that together push the story towards tragedy.

QUESTIONS & ANSWERS

This section focuses on your own analytical writing on the text, and gives you strategies for producing high-quality responses in your coursework and exam essays.

Essay writing – an overview

An essay on a literary work is a formal and serious piece of writing that presents your point of view on the text, usually in response to a given topic. Your 'point of view' in an essay is your interpretation of the meaning of the text's language, structure, characters, situations and events, supported by detailed analysis of textual evidence.

Analyse – don't summarise

In your essays it is important to avoid simply summarising what happens in a text.

- A **summary** is a description or paraphrase (retelling in different words) of the characters and events. For example: 'Macbeth has a horrifying vision of a dagger dripping with blood before he goes to murder King Duncan.'
- An **analysis** is an explanation of the real meaning or significance that lies 'beneath' the text's words (and images, for a film). For example: 'Macbeth's vision of a bloody dagger shows how deeply uneasy he is about the violent act he is contemplating, and conveys his sense that supernatural forces are impelling him to act.'

A limited amount of summary is sometimes necessary to let your reader know which part of the text you wish to discuss. However, always keep this to a minimum and follow it immediately with your analysis of what this part of the text is really telling us.

Plan your essay

Carefully plan your essay so that you have a clear idea of what you are going to say. The plan ensures that your ideas flow logically, that your argument remains consistent and that you stay on the topic. An essay plan should be a list of **brief dot points** covering no more than half a page.

- Include your central argument or main contention – a concise statement of your overall response to the topic.
- Write three or four dot points for each paragraph indicating the main idea and evidence/examples from the text. Note that in your essay you will need to *expand* on these points and *analyse* the evidence.

Structure your essay

An essay is a complete, self-contained piece of writing. It has a clear beginning (the introduction), middle (several body paragraphs) and end (the last paragraph or conclusion). It must also have a central argument that runs throughout, linking each paragraph to form a coherent whole. See examples of introductions and conclusions in the 'Analysing a Sample Topic' and 'Sample Answer' sections.

The introduction establishes your overall response to the topic. It includes your main contention and outlines the main evidence you will refer to in the course of the essay. Write your introduction *after* you have done a plan and *before* you write the rest of the essay.

The body paragraphs argue your case – they present evidence from the text and explain how this evidence supports your argument. Each body paragraph needs:

- a strong **topic sentence** (usually the first sentence) that states the main point being made in the paragraph
- **evidence** from the text, including some brief quotations
- **analysis** of the textual evidence, with explanation of its significance and how it supports your argument
- **links back to the topic** in one or more statements, usually towards the end of the paragraph.

Connect the body paragraphs so that your discussion flows smoothly. Use some linking words and phrases such as 'similarly' and 'on the other hand', though don't start every paragraph like this. Another strategy is to use a significant word from the last sentence of one paragraph in the first sentence of the next.

Use key terms from the topic – or synonyms for them – throughout, so the relevance of your discussion to the topic is always clear.

The conclusion ties everything together and finishes the essay. It includes strong statements that emphasise your central argument and provide a clear response to the topic.

Avoid simply restating the points made earlier in the essay – this will end on a very flat note and imply that you have run out of ideas and vocabulary. The conclusion should be a logical extension of what you have written, not just a repetition or summary of it. Writing an effective conclusion can be a challenge. Try using these tips:

- Start by linking back to the final sentence of the second-last paragraph – this helps your writing to flow, rather than leaping back to your main contention straight away.
- Use synonyms and expressions with equivalent meanings to vary your vocabulary. This allows you to reinforce your line of argument without being repetitive.
- When planning your essay, think of one or two broad statements or observations about the text's wider meaning. These should be related to the topic and your overall argument. Keep them for the conclusion, since they will give you something 'new' to say but still follow logically from your discussion. The introduction will be focused on the topic, but the conclusion can present a wider view of the text.

Essay topics

1. Explore the significance of the title, *The Man Who Loved Children*. Does Sam love his children?
2. How does sexism manifest in the novel, both in the Pollit family home and in society as a whole?
3. Louisa prepared the poisoned cup, but is she most responsible for Henny's death? If not, who is?
4. In what ways does Louisa differ from the other members of her family?
5. "Perhaps he, Samuel Clemens Pollit, was a forerunner of the truly great man." How does Sam's egotism manifest in the novel?
6. *The Man Who Loved Children* is filled with strange dialects and songs, poems and quotations. How do these different modes of communication contribute to our view of at least *two* characters?
7. Women seem to be doomed in the world of the novel, at least according to Henny. Is her pessimism justified, or is there hope of escape from misery for the female characters?
8. How does Sam's idealism affect the Pollit family, including Sam himself?
9. Henny and Sam's rivalry is at the centre of the novel. Why does Henny resent her husband so vehemently?
10. What is the significance of Sam's trip to Malaya, and what does it reveal about his character?

Vocabulary for writing on *The Man Who Loved Children*

Bildungsroman: a term of German origin to describe a novel that focuses on a young character's transition from childhood to adulthood.

Free indirect speech: a style of writing that describes third-person narration that slips in and out of describing particular characters' thoughts, feelings and ideas.

Irony: a device or technique in which the implied meaning of a statement or idea contrasts with its literal meaning or effect. For example, in *The Man Who Loved Children*, Sam articulates many theories of ideal government and society, while creating misery and disorder in his own house. This contrast is *ironic*.

Symbol: an object with a deeper meaning or representational function beyond itself. Stead is not a deeply symbolic writer; however, as an example of her use of symbolism, the animals kept in cages in the Pollit house can be seen as representative of the confinement of several of the novel's female characters.

Analysing a sample topic

Explore the significance of the title, *The Man Who Loved Children*. Does Sam love his children?

This question asks you to interrogate the meaning of the novel's title, focusing especially on the character of Sam and his relationship to his children. Note that you are asked to explain the 'significance' of the title, so you should aim to link the title to broader *themes* articulated in the novel. The title of an artistic work is often a brief but very significant clue to its key thematic interests. Useful initial questions to ask might include why the author has chosen this particular title and whether it gels with your perceptions after having read the work – and why or why not. Importantly, you should direct your observations towards forming a cogent response on what you think the title means.

If the title is mentioned within the text itself, revisit that passage to see if it offers any 'clues' for analysis. Henny uses the titular phrase in an argument with Sam on page 138. Sam is afraid that Henny will turn the children against him, and only bitterly concedes that they are Henny's children as well. Henny calls Sam 'the man who loves children' in derision. In light of this, the title seems to tap into Sam's narcissism, since there is more than one person in the novel who 'loves' these children.

In focusing on key words, you should also give careful thought to any words that might be contentious in terms of their definition. Here, how you define 'love' will be important and could lead you to a variety of perspectives. Sam is certainly selfish, but perhaps his love for his children is a redeeming quality? Alternatively, maybe he loves his children, but does not express that love in an ideal way? Another approach might suggest that Sam's selfishness disqualifies him from truly 'loving' his children, since he refuses to allow them (especially Louisa) an identity beyond what he defines for them. Another approach might accept the use of the word 'love' but concede that Sam's love is ultimately directed at bolstering his own power and ego. Thus, the answer to this question depends significantly on how you interpret the contentious word 'love'.

Furthermore, today, in an era of increased awareness of child sexual abuse, a more sinister dimension to the title is inevitably more pronounced. Sam does not sexually abuse his children, but the spectre of abuse is certainly present throughout the novel. This knowledge may dramatically alter how you view the word 'love'. Whereas the lines of analysis above largely attribute positive value to the word, if you imply that that 'love' contains an erotic dimension, then there is a sinister interpretation. Perhaps Sam does indeed 'love' his children, but inappropriately. Following this line of argument would mean you need to provide examples in the novel in which Sam's 'love' for children appears inappropriate (e.g. his preference for younger female children).

With any essay, the response needs to be organised into paragraphs that explain and prove the overall point or 'argument'. It is imperative that that argument respond to the question by explaining your interpretation of the title, and clearly indicate whether you believe Sam truly 'loves' his children.

Sample introduction

> The title of Stead's novel clearly indicates the importance of Sam's relationship to his children in the text: he is 'The Man Who Loved Children'. There is little doubt that Sam

is greatly attached to his children, but he also generates considerable misery for them, especially his eldest daughter, Louisa. This calls into question whether he truly 'loves' them. The title of the novel is intended to be ironic: while superficially it depicts Sam in a positive light, in actuality his fatherly love is self-centred and destructive. Sam uses his children to enhance his own ego; moreover, his affection for his children allows him to shirk responsibility by remaining 'childlike' himself. In general, Sam's 'love' for his children is so wrapped up in his own power that the term 'love' cannot be easily accepted, and the title of the novel highlights the superficiality of Sam's virtue.

Body paragraph outline

Paragraph 1: Sam's love for his children is primarily about feeding his own ego.

- Sam demonstrates great affection for children at many points in the text; however, the sincerity of the novel's title is undermined by the extent to which Sam's 'love' seems to focus on his own ego.
- Sam's egotistical interest in children is demonstrated when he expresses his strange desire to father numerous children of various races (p.210), casting himself as an all-powerful father to all.
- With his homemade dialect, Sam creates a world with his children in which he is forever the leader of the gang. He broadcasts his ideas and theories to them, a safe and adoring audience, as a way of increasing his own importance.
- When gossip begins to circulate about Sam, it becomes clear that he does not actually have many adult friends; he is quite dependent on the children – even parasitically (especially in Louie's case).
- In light of this, Sam's love for his children is tied to bolstering his own importance. He may indeed 'love children' but that love is ultimately about retaining power.

Paragraph 2: Sam's love of children is partly about remaining 'childlike'.

- Sam is depicted as childlike at numerous points throughout the novel, allowing us to see that his close relationship with his children is substantially about remaining 'childlike' himself.
- His use of a childlike dialect allows him to 'play' at being a child.
- Sam's childish behaviour is also demonstrated in his game-playing with his sister on page 327, and in his impudent demanding of bananas on page 474, among many other instances.
- This 'childlike' nature obscures his power; being 'childlike' is a way of playing innocent despite the damage he causes, allowing him to shirk responsibility.
- Thus, the title's significance is also partly that Sam doesn't merely 'love' children, he loves wallowing in his own immaturity. His supposed 'love' for his children involves his wilful ignorance and is, again, ultimately focused on himself.

Paragraph 3: Sam's supposed 'love' for his children is controlling and stifles their individuality.

- The nature of Sam's love for his children involves considerable control, compromising their individuality and raising the question of whether his attachment to them can be called 'loving' without irony.
- Sam is afraid of female influence on his children, indicated by his refusal to have Hazel Moore, Henny's former housekeeper, in the house while he is away; this reflects his need to control his children.
- He is also terrified by Louisa's adolescence, scared that she might develop an identity that he does not prescribe or control. On page 322, he nearly demonises her ('a stern, selfish vain nature'), indicating his investment in who she becomes.
- Sam's controlling, even bullying, nature is also demonstrated when he mocks Louisa's appearance as she dances (p.113). When his children fight, Sam ignores Little-Sam's plea that the fight be stopped (p.83); and when carrying the marlin offal makes Little-Sam want to vomit, Sam forces him to continue carrying it (p.480). None of this is the behaviour of a truly loving father.

Paragraph 4: Sam's love for children has a disturbing sexual dimension.

- Although Sam does not commit any acts of sexual abuse within the novel, the suggestion that his 'love' of children has a repressed sexual dimension means we cannot read the title without irony.
- Sam is drawn to young girls; on pages 44 and 45 he tries to attract neighbourhood children to the house, preferring young girls.
- He is attracted to Gillian Roebuck, the young daughter of a colleague, whom he sees as a 'child-woman' (p.16).
- Sam is whipped into a defensive frenzy upon hearing about a local father accused of abusing his teenage daughter, suggesting that he identifies with the father (p.371).
- This trips a wave of hatred from Louisa towards her father, because she recognises in the incident a disturbing similarity with his cloying and controlling approach to her. This is explored in the play she writes, 'Herpes Rom', about an incestuous father and his daughter.

Sample conclusion

> Sam's devotion to his children is a significant feature of Stead's novel, but it is not a character trait we can accept unquestioningly. Close analysis reveals that the title is saturated with irony that exposes Sam's love as self-centred and even exploitative. Sam 'loves' his children because they offer him an avenue to maintain his sense of power, and only insofar as they fulfil the roles he expects of them. He is brought into conflict with Louisa precisely because he will not allow her to be her own person, rather than a subservient facsimile of himself. Sam's intrusion on his daughter's life and his attraction to childish women also lends an uncomfortable sexual dimension to the title. The seemingly 'positive' description of Sam in the title urges us to carefully consider the nature of the 'love' depicted in the novel, and to unearth the ways in which that love falls short.

SAMPLE ANSWER

In what ways does Louisa differ from the other members of her family?

The sensitive and introverted Louisa is a central character in *The Man Who Loved Children*. She is the individual whose thoughts we are granted most access to, and the only member of the Pollit household who ultimately breaks away to create a different life for herself. While Louisa has several things in common with other members of her family, this essay will explain three key ways in which she stands out: her artistic abilities and ambitions, her ability to see through her father's controlling behaviour, and her rejection of her prescribed gender role in order to create a different life for herself.

From the first pages of Stead's novel, Louisa stands out for her imaginative and artistic personality. In the first chapter, as she tries to sleep, she pictures a 'night rider' outside, her imaginative rendering of what turns out to be the blood in her own temples. At school she writes many poems, and eventually composes an elaborate cycle of poems in honour of her favourite teacher. Louisa shares this interest in language with Sam, who devises numerous songs and poems throughout the course of the novel, including when we first meet him. However, whereas Sam's spontaneous poems are frivolous, often cruel and only superficially inventive, Louisa's artistic productions are mature, sensitive and serious-minded. Her artistic and imaginative ability is accompanied by a hidden reservoir of self-confidence; in Chapter Two, she feels she is a 'genius'. Like Henny, Louisa is beaten down by Sam. However, whereas Henny collapses into despair or explodes with bitterness, Louisa's faith in her creative talents allows her to remain fixated on a better future for herself. Consequently, her artistic and imaginative abilities are important features of her character, distinguishing her from others in the family.

Louisa is also distinguished by being the only Pollit child to see through Sam's happy-go-lucky persona and glimpse the manipulative nature beneath. She challenges her father's power at various points in the novel, indicating her refusal to accept his views. Her questioning begins in the first chapter, and is thus an important introduction to her character. While Sam expects his daughter to be aligned with him, Louisa starts to see her stepmother differently and begins to understand Henny's hostility to Sam. Similarly, although Sam often takes Louisa aside, confiding in her and giving advice, Louisa recognises that her father is only seeking to mould her in his image: 'you're always trying to make me think like you: I can't'. There is evidence that children other than Louisa are not happy in the house (e.g. Ernie's hangman's noose), but Louisa is the only child who has a consistent awareness of her father's controlling personality, a trait for which she stands out.

Another important way in which Louisa distinguishes herself is through her rejection of gender roles. Her artistic ambitions mean she challenges what is expected of a young woman during the period in which she lives; and her rejection of her father's views also involves rejecting what he expects of her. As mentioned above, Louisa writes love poems, despite having no female literary role models and little encouragement of her work. Within the Pollit house, Louisa's prescribed role involves stereotypically female duties of cooking and cleaning – she seems to do the majority of the housework. While Evie continues to take pride and interest in performing such roles at the end of the novel, Louisa rejects them completely: instead of making breakfast, she leaves. Moreover, her quest beyond the Pollit house is not a search for a more ideal male figure, but a journey to fulfil her own destiny and potential. Louisa's successful rejection of male-prescribed roles is unique in the novel; Henny is also dissatisfied with her role but she is trapped until her death. Indeed, it might even be argued that Louisa's role in Henny's death represents not just her putting her mother out of her misery, but is also a symbolic rejection of the suffocated and worn-down maternal role Henny represents.

Both the first and final chapters of Stead's novel conclude by focusing on Louisa, indicating the importance of her character to the novel. She is the one who is able to hold to her ambitions and escape the suffocating influence of 'Pollitry'. In pursuing her independence, the traits noted above are of considerable importance. Her artistic ability gives her insight and self-confidence, and her ability to see through her father and reject the gender roles he endorses pushes her to finally break free.

REFERENCES & READING

Text

Stead, Christina 2011, *The Man Who Loved Children,* The Miegunyah Press, Melbourne. First published in 1940.

Books and journal articles

Brydon, Diana 1987, *Christina Stead,* Macmillan Education, Basingstoke.

Clancy, Laurie 1981, *Christina Stead's* The Man Who Loved Children *and* For Love Alone, Shillington House, Melbourne.

Gardiner, Judith Kegan 2000, 'Male Narcissism, Capitalism, and the Daughter of *The Man Who Loved Children*', in Margaret Harris (ed.), *The Magic Phrase: Critical Essays on Christina Stead,* University of Queensland Press, St Lucia, pp.145–62.

Lidoff, Joan 1982, *Christina Stead,* Frederick Ungar, New York.

Rowley, Hazel 1993, *Christina Stead: a biography,* Heinemann, Sydney.

Stern, Kate Macomber 1989, *Christina Stead's Heroine: The Changing Sense of Decorum,* Peter Lang, New York.

Walker, Shirley 2000, 'Language, Art and Ideas in *The Man Who Loved Children*', in Margaret Harris (ed.), *The Magic Phrase: Critical Essays on Christina Stead,* University of Queensland Press, St Lucia, pp.117–32.

Newspaper articles

Smiley, Jane 2006, 'Dangerous Excesses', *The Guardian,* 10 June, www.theguardian.com/books/2006/jun/10/featuresreviews.guardianreview29

Websites

Scheidenhelm, Carol 2007, 'American Literary History: Romanticism, Realism and Naturalism', Loyola University Chicago, 14 August, www.luc.edu/faculty/cschei1/teach/rrn3.html

'*The Man Who Loved Children* by Christina Stead' 2011, *The Book Club*, ABC, 5 April, www.abc.net.au/tv/firsttuesday/s3141570.htm